PURSUING LIBERTY

AMERICA THROUGH THE
EYES OF THE NEWLY FREE

CORY EMBERSON & RICK LINDSTROM

Founders Editions

California

PURSUING LIBERTY

AMERICA THROUGH THE EYES OF THE NEWLY FREE

Founders Editions
California

Cover by Laura Bowly Design

Grateful acknowledgment is made to *Investor's Business Daily* for permission to reprint "The Perspective of a Russian Immigrant" by Svetlana Kunin.

ISBN 978-0-9826966-1-3

PRINTED IN THE UNITED STATES OF AMERICA

DEDICATION

To my son Chris, with much love and admiration, and to his fellow Americans by birth and by choice who give their all for American liberty.

— CE

To Beebo and Ya, and especially to those who have and will put their lives on the line to bequeath liberty to future American generations.

— RL

If we lose freedom here, there is no place to escape to.
This is the last stand on Earth.
— RONALD WILSON REAGAN

ACKNOWLEDGMENTS

THE CREATION OF *Pursuing Liberty* was singularly reliant on the contributions of others. To each American by choice who generously took the time to relate in great and often painful detail your experiences living under repression, your appreciation of the shining city of American exceptionalism, and for your thoughtful reflection of current events, you have our profound gratitude and admiration. Thank you.

Our thanks, too, to Gregory Poulos for your careful vetting of the historical information contained in each chapter, your precision of language, and love for our country.

Thank you to fellow aviator and friend Allen Wolpert for your advice, support, and belief in this project.

And thank you to each person – American by birth or by choice – who urged us to press on with this book, so these narratives, representative of millions of others from all over the world, will not be forgotten.

CONTENTS

PROLOGUE

THE STORIES YOU ARE about to read are true. The words come right from the American immigrants who were interviewed for this project, and who were graciously forthcoming in sharing their personal and sometimes painful experiences. Although we did ask them questions during the interviews from time to time, they were not coached or urged to take political positions in any way. These are their stories as told to us, as close to verbatim as possible.

To be put in printed form, some light editing was needed for clarity and flow, however, very little has been changed from the original narratives. For those who are used to reading finely crafted literature, where words and thoughts seem to flow seamlessly, these narratives may seem choppy or a bit rough. This is intentional, as we wanted to avoid putting any unintended coloration in these stories by the normal editing process, or to remove the genuine flavor of their words.

By delivering these narratives in as close to original form as possible, we trust that you, the reader, will appreciate the power and veracity of these words, as spoken by those who own them. We hope that readers will also be able to read between the lines, and get a sense of the emotions that bubbled forth as these immigrants recalled their personal experiences.

We prefaced each personal story with some historical background of their birth countries to provide some political and social context for each person's narrative. Some of this historical background may be familiar; some may be a revelation. We hope this brief taste will encourage you to explore their histories in more detail. Some histories date from the earliest signs of man in the region; some only focus on a specific window of time. In all cases, they're intended only to give a bit of background to the following narratives, and should not be considered comprehensive in nature.

Although it's been years since these immigrants fled tyranny in their birth countries, some were hesitant to speak as frankly as they would've liked, even now. Some requested that their true identities be obscured, for fear of retaliation against relatives still living under repressive regimes.

Some might deduce that this book was written with an agenda of bashing our current federal administration, given that many of our interviewees are so critical of the country's current political direction. Please understand the extreme concern of these new Americans, in some cases absolutely terrified that their new country will devolve into the very misery they left behind. They have a valid point, given their first hand experiences.

We hope that you find these stories as inspirational we have, as you see our country through the eyes of those who have pursued liberty to the point of leaving everything they knew to become our newest proud Americans.

Cory Emberson
Rick Lindstrom
2010

FOREWORD

My HEART'S PURSUIT OF LIBERTY was born in 1906 – the year my grandfather immigrated to the United States from Russia. The blood-red seeds of Communist tyranny had sprouted a year earlier during the St. Petersburg Massacre, and his parents – my great-grandparents – realized that radical, life-changing circumstances were imminent.

I'm told that in a moment of hopeful desperation, my great-grandparents instructed their eldest son, David, with this charge: "Go to America. Earn money. Send for your brother."

David was thirteen. He boarded a ship, landed at Ellis Island, and somehow managed his way to Philadelphia to briefly live with relatives. Unable to speak English, he was urged by his hosts to respond to a newspaper ad; a local firm had an opening for a door-to-door junk peddler. Hundreds of young people showed up to apply, but only a few were chosen; one of those was young David.

David soon discovered he had a knack for sales. He quickly learned English, worked hard, faithfully sent for his brother, married a lovely Russian immigrant bride, became a successful businessman, and together they raised four children – one, of course, being my dad. Sadly I never met my grandmother; she died when her children were still very young. However, rather than allowing his life and family to fall into an emotional tailspin, David dug into the promise of America. In doing so, he never forgot his roots and always warned his children of the poison of tyranny – a wicked blight that would eventually claim the lives of his family members in the old country.

The legacy of my grandfather was resident within the life of my dad. Dad loved America and its promise of Life, Liberty, and the Pursuit of Happiness. He always had a heart for the honest immigrant and possessed great respect for those who came here to work hard and prosper. He loved our free-market system of economics and despised government in-tervention. He and my mother lived within their means, saved for their future, and yet always donned nice clothing, drove a sharp-looking car, and raised my brother and me in a comfortable, well-appointed home. And, like most men from his era, Dad was willing to defend the promises of America, even at the risk of his own life.

Within the pages of this inspirational book, you will read modern-day examples of people very much like my grand-father – men and women who immigrated to this country, desperate to taste the virtues of freedom. As a conservative radio talk-show host in a very diverse region, I often con-verse with such individuals as they call in to my program.

"Do you understand what is happening to *our* country?" they plead with their strong accents.

Others say, "America must wake up and not allow social-ism to take hold."

One particularly emotional caller from the former Soviet Union proclaimed, "The United States is the last beacon of freedom. We cannot allow it to fall."

Pursuing Liberty is a book that reminds us of the wisdom of our Founders, and inspires us through the stories of our newest patriots.

—Brian Sussman, KSFO,
San Francisco radio host,
and author of *Climategate.*

PURSUING LIBERTY

One

SOVIET UNION

*"When I look at the aspirations of American Progressives,
I see nothing new or forward-looking. Instead, I see the same
ideas that formed the basis of the USSR, which
eventually suffered a complete economic collapse."*

*Svetlana (right) and her sister in the Soviet
Union one month before she and her family
emigrated to the United States, 1980.*

Soviet Union

RUSSIAN HISTORY IS SKETCHY at best up until the 7th century, when Slavic tribes settled in the valley between the Baltic, Black, Caspian, and White Seas. In 862, the first Slavic state was founded when a Scandinavian warrior named Rurik led his people to the city of Novgorod on the Volkhov River, and later his successor Oleg gained control of Kiev on the Dnepr River. This area became known as Kievan Rus', united with most of the neighboring Slavic lands, all practicing an orthodox form of Christianity imported from Byzantium.

Over the next two hundred years, the formerly united Kievan Rus' gave way to aggressive, independent principalities that fell one by one to the Mongol invasion that claimed them all except the Republic of Novgorod. The autocracy of the Mongols had a profound influence on the local culture, with an inclination toward collective thought instead of individual action.

In 1303, a Russian prince named Daniil inherited a tiny principality at the confluence of the Neglina and Moskva Rivers. This small outpost had the advantage of being the focus of several trade routes, and the city of Moscow grew and ultimately became a regional power. In 1480, the Russians of Moscow battled the Mongols, defeated them, and became an independent state. By the 16th century, the rulers in Moscow had effectively consolidated the surrounding ethnically Russian lands, and began expanding even further.

This expansion came with a price, however, as the rulers in Moscow failed to have a workable strategy for the unification and development of the expanding state. Civil war and chaos reigned from 1598 to 1613 as many Russians competed for the crown, and other wars upon Russia were declared by Poland and Sweden. Mikhail Romanov prevailed in 1613 as the new Russian czar, thus beginning a 304-year Romanov reign, until the Russian Revolution brought an end to the czars.

In 1812, Napoleon desired to add Russia to a long list of other European countries under his control, but underestimated the tenacity of the Russian soldiers and the intensity of the Russian winters. In mid-October, the French army began the long march home after a failed invasion, during which it was decimated from cold and starvation. In 1825, a group of reformist military officers (known as the Decembrists) attempted, and failed, at forcing a constitutional monarchy into being. In 1861, however, one of the many political parties opposed to czarist rule organized in Minsk as the RSDRP, or the Russian Social-Democratic Party. Later on, they began to refer to themselves simply as Communists.

Following the defeat from the war with Japan in 1906 and weary from World War I, Russia's social fabric was already torn when Czar Nicholas II was forced to abdicate in early 1917. Plans were to move the royal family to England, but that plan was overruled by the Bolsheviks. Nicholas and his entire family were taken to Yekaterinaburg, where they were murdered by Lenin's directive, and their bodies were disposed of down an unused mine shaft. By autumn, and under the guidance of Vladimir Lenin, radical Bolsheviks began to eliminate all vestiges of the former government. After a period of civil strife that devastated the country, the Russian Revolution came to an end as the Bolsheviks finally prevailed in 1920.

After Lenin's death in 1924, a power struggle ensued within the Communist Party. Joseph Stalin emerged victorious at the end of the decade, and began a campaign of tighter controls over all facets of Russian life.

In spite of a non-aggression pact signed with Germany in 1939, Russia found itself being invaded by Hitler's forces in June of 1941. In November 1942, Russian forces began fighting back successfully against the German army, ultimately pushing the Germans back to Poland in 1944. On May 2, 1945, Berlin fell to the Russians.

Stalin remained in power until he died of a brain hemorrhage in 1953. Soviet Russia's rigid society was then led by a succession of Cold War period leaders, Nikita Khrushchev, Leonid Brezhnev, Yuri Andropov, and Konstantin Chernenko up until 1985. When Mikhail Gorbachev became general secretary in March of 1986, the policy of *glasnost* (openness) was introduced, and social reforms began in earnest.

In 1989, the first open elections were held since 1917, giving voters a choice of more than a single candidate. In 1990, the old Soviet Union began to fall, with its former satellite countries gaining independence one by one. By the end of the year, the former Soviet Union had been voted out of existence, Gorbachev resigned, and the Soviet hammer and sickle flag was finally replaced with the traditional Russian tricolor flag.

Svetlana Kunin

"The Soviet economic structure resulted in low productivity, stagnation, outdated technology, and the suppression of creativity and individual initiative."

MY FATHER BELIEVED IN SOCIALISM: the beautiful slogans of fairness and equality, sacrifice and service to the country. They were part of the Soviet society, and my father became a member of the Communist Party right before he went to war in 1939. He was born two years before the 1917 Socialist Revolution in Russia, and my mother was born in 1918; they lived in a little town in Russia.

In 1939, right after graduation from law school in Minsk, my father was drafted into the Soviet Army, and my parents got married right before the war started between the Soviet Union and Germany. He fought in World War II from 1939 until 1945. In 1944, he came home for three months to get treatment for his war wounds, and he received medals of valor. My sister was born in 1940, my brother was born in 1944, and I was born in 1949.

After the war he worked as a corporate lawyer, and my mother worked as a librarian. We lived in a two-room apartment in Minsk. It was a separate apartment; unlike many families, we did not share a kitchen with any other families, and we had our own bathroom. This was considered pretty good conditions.

We were Jewish, but we were a very assimilated family. After the Revolution all religions were eliminated. As a child, if you had a religious parent, you wouldn't mention that in school because it would be embarrassing. My parents were not religious, but my father looked like a very ethnic Jewish man. When I was eleven I witnessed some teenagers insulting him right in front of me. My father did nothing. I was naïve, because my parents protected my life. You live your life as a child – you have your friends, and you go through your routine like everybody else.

With time, my father began to understand that the ideals and realities of socialism weren't the same. He was a long-time member of the Communist Party, and was faithful to the country. It was very difficult for him to realize that idea was flawed. Superiority of the proletariat was the slogan. The reality was the superiority of the Communist Party.

Constant propaganda surrounded us. From nursery school through college, we were told how great our country was, and how scary the world of capitalism is. People adapted to the surrounding conditions. We were quite accustomed to standing in line for everything: food, clothes, furniture. We grabbed what was offered. In a way it was easier – we didn't have to choose. Usually nobody complained, because that's the way it was. We had friends, we lived, we cried, we loved, got married. And if someone asked if we loved our country – the majority were very patriotic. People in the USSR didn't have any opportunity to travel outside of the country. All information came through the government-controlled media.

The only source of outside information that some people, like my father, could obtain was Voice of America and the

BBC, transmitted in Russian. This information was quite different.

We grew up, went to college, and started our own lives. I was a civil engineer and my husband was an electrical engineer. Except for changes in fashion and the slow introduction of new technological improvement such as television and washing machines, our lives very much reflected the lives of our parents. But my father never told us that not everything was as good as it was presented. The Russian system was like a welfare society. Everyone works, and compensation is just enough to cover basic necessities.

There was a shortage of everything, including places to live. So, young couples usually started their lives in their parents' apartment, and registered on the waiting list to get their own apartment. To get an apartment in Russia, you either had to bribe somebody or wait for many years to get your own apartment. For five years we lived with my parents – it took five to ten years to get an apartment. If you wanted to move to another city, you had to find a place to live. Because of the shortage of living space everywhere, it was almost impossible to move to another city for better opportunities. People lived where they were assigned to live.

By the time my husband and I were thirty years old in 1979, we realized that we had reached our ceiling. There was no way to better our life. Religion was suppressed, but people were divided by ethnicity: Russian, Belarussian, Jewish. There was constant tension between the ethnic groups in the USSR.

As my husband and I experienced adulthood, we realized how little control we had over our destiny. We could not change our jobs because of the widespread government-approved anti-Semitism. Once or twice a year we were sent away from the family for a month to collective agricultural farms to help harvest crops. Nobody cared that people had children and didn't want to leave them for a month, and many didn't have anyone to leave their children with. We were just masses, with little space for our own lives, limited by assigned boundaries. And if the government required you to serve – you had to serve.

The biggest danger and struggle everyone faced was if someone got seriously sick. You can get used to standing in lines and can adapt to a limited food supply. But if you or someone you loved needed serious medical care – this is when the real misery starts. When a person got sick and checked into the hospital, the relatives were not allowed to visit. They could bring food and pass it through the receptionist. The conditions were unsanitary, and painkiller medication, as everything else, was in short supply. This is where bribery and begging for help took place. If you were lucky, you survived, got out, and continued your life, with just horrific memories of your experience of government-controlled medical care... otherwise, you died.

The former USSR was rich with natural resources, but because central government-controlled enterprises are very inefficient and corrupt, the agricultural output was very low. In 1970 the country experienced a famine, and was forced to buy grain from outside sources.

I wasn't part of the Russian dissident movement, like Natan Sharansky was. Dissidents started to fight for individual and religious freedoms. They passed information to foreign visitors about their movement and struggle. At that time, Soviet dissidents, through the number of courageous foreign visitors from America and some European countries, passed information to the world outside of the Iron Curtain. This way, information about political prisoners, religious persecution, and government-supported anti-Semitism was exposed.

Henry "Scoop" Jackson was an anti-Communist Senator from the state of Washington, and introduced the Jackson-Vanik Amendment in 1974 to allow the sale of agricultural products to the USSR, with the condition that Jews and political dissidents would be allowed to leave the Soviet Union if they wanted. This was a miracle, I would say.

We had a chance to change our lives, and we took it. We had to resign from our jobs, pay huge amounts of money for exit visas, relinquish our citizenship, and our parents had to give us permission to leave. Out of all our relatives and friends, only my father said we made the right move. We left everything behind in 1980, and knew we would never see them again. Our son was eight at the time.

A lot of our brainwashed relatives didn't understand us. They were afraid to be around us. My husband and I understood that in Russia, we were nothing. We were like a little nail in the big mechanism – whatever wrong move we made, we would be crushed.

And only my father, who served the Soviet Union for his entire life but was more informed than the others, supported our decision. He lent us his life savings for the period when we were hanging in limbo without jobs, waiting for permission to leave the country. He paid a price for that.

My father was still working, and still a member of the Communist Party. It was his life, but he knew it would be better for us to leave. Ten years after we left, I found out that he went through a show meeting, was expelled from the Party, and was forced to retire. Because we left, the Party ruined his life.

We never saw him again. In 1985 he was given the wrong treatment in the hospital, and died screaming from pain for three days until his death, while my mother and sister were not allowed to see him.

When we came to the United States, we already had permission to live and work in America. We had three hundred dollars, three suitcases, some clothes, two pillows, and a few blankets. Some people shipped furniture. We didn't, we just left. We were sponsored by HIAS, the Hebrew Immigrant Aid Society, a private charitable organization. They lent us money for six months for rent and food until we found jobs.

We were grateful and actually amazed that there were such charities that helped people in need. With all the slogans of fairness and justice for all, we never experienced charity or sympathy from strangers who didn't have to care about us. My husband, while working full time, went back to Johns Hopkins University to get his degree in computer science. I took several courses in computer science, and in one year I found my first programming job.

My husband found a job in about five months. Whatever job we found, we took. We were very happy when we got our first jobs, and we didn't expect any help. I was doing data entry for $4.50 an hour and my husband found a position as an electronic technician for $8 an hour at Martin Marietta. When we started working, we repaid our loan to the HIAS. We bought a 1972 Dodge Coronet for $450 and felt very lucky.

I hear people complaining how bad the American social system is. If this is such an unfair country, why are people from all over the world trying to get here? Is there any other country in the world where immigrants have such an opportunity to obtain a better life for themselves and their families as the United States? And if immigrants can do it, why is it citizens who were born here can't? Why do minority students only know about Reverend Al Sharpton, but the lives of such outstanding people like Justice Clarence Thomas, Thomas Sowell, and professor Walter Williams are not case studies in every school of America? Why is such an enormously ignorant and dishonest movie producer as Michael Moore celebrated by progressive political leaders?

When we came to the U.S. in 1980, it was the last year of Jimmy Carter's presidency. There was a terrible recession, but we didn't know that it was a recession. The stores were full of groceries. The first time I went to the store, I almost fainted, with all the nice smells, bananas and oranges. I never saw so many things you could buy in my entire life.

Only members of the government and the small group of elites had access to stores with good supplies. If once or twice a year I could buy oranges, I would give the oranges to my son so he would have something healthful to eat and I would eat the white rind. Even a pineapple... I didn't know what it was. Apples, of course, we knew because they grew there – not through the whole year, only in season.

When we came here my son only knew two sentences: "I don't speak English" and "Where is a bathroom?" By his second year in America he didn't have any problems. Who is pushing bilingual education? Why? The school's business is to teach children to live and work in America. And the family can decide if they need to keep their traditions.

In 1985 my husband graduated from college and gained more experience. Our lifestyle was getting better and better. By the time of Mikhail Gorbachev's Perestroika in 1987, my father had already died. I never got to see him again.

The majority of the people got used to doing what they were told. Russia was a very closed society. What you're told in schools or on TV is all you know, unless you have access to the Voice of America or some underground literature. A lot of nationalistic movements started. Anti-Semitism was open and ugly, and Jews were afraid for their lives. We sponsored our relatives so they could leave the USSR to come to the U.S.

There were some things I didn't like when I came to America, specifically education in the public schools. The way teachers' unions are destroying the educational system in America is criminal. The schools do not teach modern history of the world. People don't know history – not only children, but also adults! I don't think the level of education is sufficient, especially in history, math, science, and reading. They should encourage children to be curious people. What they teach isn't enough for a country with such a high level of technology.

There generally isn't much substance in history classes, no in-depth analysis of why events happened the way they did. Education is so important... people don't have a real level of understanding of even their own country, how it evolved, how it compares to other countries, how it's different from every other country in the world.

This leads me to why I wrote the column for *Investor's Business Daily*. What I see happening now reminds me of what I saw and escaped from in the USSR. The same socialist slogans and criticism of capitalism are on display in front of our eyes in the United States. Many Americans don't have the perspective of what people are free to do in America.

Why is it that so many people from different countries are *trying* to get to America? Look at the number of people who want to come here, versus the number who want to leave – and there's no restriction for law-abiding citizens who want to leave the country.

You hear so much critique of this country – well, every country can be criticized. You can find imperfections everywhere. We were educated professionals in the Soviet Union, we were doing the best we could with our jobs, and could barely afford any normal necessities.

Then we came to America, with our imperfect conversational language. When we came to America, I started to read only in English, to make myself integrate better. We started from the bottom and gradually improved our lives to become middle class. Our older son graduated from Princeton, and our younger son, who was born here, graduated from NYU. We can travel, and we live a full life here. You just cannot compare life in America to any other countries. How do people who live here not understand this?

I'd like to tell people who don't understand the difference between America and any other country is when you think about something that you'd like to criticize here, also think about how much you can appreciate here. Think about your freedom of movement, or even buying power – what you can get here. If you're from a poor family, as we were when we came here, look around and see what steps you can take to get a little bit better than where you are now.

The first step is, find any job, then you will improve your life a little bit more, and then you can think about what you like to do. If you don't have enough money to go to a university, you can go to a vocational school or community college. Get some opportunity to advance you a little further than where you are. With every new step, you can gain more and more opportunities. This country allows this.

We have cousins who live in Canada, Israel, and Germany, and another friend who lives in Australia. We were all at a gathering and talking about life. They all love their countries, but we're at a higher level than they are. Our children are better off than their children. Life is not easy anywhere, but America gives you so many opportunities.

The direction that America is taking now scares me. The government pushes for ever more control over private enterprise. People will lose opportunities. This scares me.

I think people lose their independent drive and spirit when that happens. Government has a lot of power to dictate the structure of the country, what companies should and shouldn't do. They suppress people's spirits, and their drive for accomplishment.

After the Revolution, farmers who were entrepreneurs and hard workers had others working for them. When the socialistic revolution took place, they sent people who owned businesses or farms to gulags, and left only those who worked for the rich people. As a result, a huge famine started, because the workers who were left didn't have the knowledge or initiative to actually produce.

People were starving. Then Lenin's government allowed some private initiatives to take place. It was called the National Economic Policy. They introduced some capitalism, and allowed people to have their farms, plant their own grains, and raise their own stock. This way, they eliminated hunger and poverty. Then they confiscated all properties and nationalized everything again.

This also happened in Zimbabwe. They all go through the same routine. I hope nothing like that happens to America. If you have more control in the government, and less control with the people, and you force the majority of people to work for the government, you're suppressing initiative, and the whole country becomes poor.

When I wrote my first column, I said using government medical services destroys your dignity. Many people adapt to the societies they live in. But if you live in a free country, and you didn't know there could be a structure imposed over you, and somebody imposed this structure – well, that's what's happening now. Somebody imposes a new structure over your life. You may adapt to it. It will destroy your freedom, but you will adapt. The medical care is the final step. You won't adapt – you'll just be sick. You may get better, or you will die. And there is no way for you to escape if government has control over it. That's the end of your life.

I think it would be the biggest crime if that happened in America. Those who are sick, they will be desperate.

Unfortunately, people will willingly give up their independence to a government, which is supposed to be the people's servant – not the other way around. People want somebody to make their life easier. They want somebody to give up their wealth and give it to them, or to somebody else. Okay, you do that. Then what? One person will become a little poorer, and one will become a little richer. And then what? Will he become rich after that? How many people will you find to take from, and then give to somebody? Where will it end? This is not the way for progress. This is not how a better life works, not from envy.

In order for you to achieve something, you may have a little less, or a little more than somebody else. It's not right to take from somebody else – you need to accomplish what *you* want to do. Envy doesn't drive this. Self-interest and self-reliance does.

I think President Reagan understood the nature of people. People were very impressed with the presentations during the 2008 Summer Olympics in China. There were hundreds and hundreds of people beating their drums all at the same time. A lot of people were so impressed with it. I was horrified. This is exactly the symbol of socialism. These are not people – they beat their drums to the lights: light on, light off, light on, light off. They are a part of this huge, huge machine where there is nothing unique about them. They beat the drums and march in the same order. It's symbolic.

When Obama campaigned, you could see and hear this very cushioned repetition of "it's not fair," "you need to do this for the greater good." It was like in the USSR: the same slogans, and the murals on the walls. When I came to America, I was surprised to see people's ignorance. Russia was a mystery to them – they adored the country. There was a lack of information about the USSR, what the country was about.

Now, Russian society has opened to capitalism. It may take a few generations for the Russian people to become accustomed to freedom, because they couldn't make those decisions for themselves for so long.

I visited the apartment building where I grew up, and it's exactly the same. It's the same slow-moving life. When I spoke with my friend, she couldn't imagine how much better I am in America than she is in Russia.

This is the way my generation lives. It's like still life. Younger people in Russia don't even remember life before Perestroika. They have more initiative, they're more optimistic, they *look* different. So, there's a chance that in several generations, it will change. When you open a society, they will progress. They will change when they are free.

This administration always has a scapegoat. First, the investment bankers, then the insurance companies, then rich people, then car manufacturers, then Republicans, Tea Party people, then radio and TV commentators. They stir up their supporters and radicalize them. In order to maintain this hatred, they invent new villains. How else can you transform the country? You can create a need in people for change, and it doesn't matter what the change is.

They see someone who's rich, and they're told that they're rich because they took it from you. So, they try to destroy someone who is sticking out, who is exceptional. They project it to the insurance companies, or Wall Street, and then they just suppress information that would contradict what they've done. The final goal of what they're doing is taking control of society more and more. The latest scapegoating is against regular people of both parties going to town hall meetings and Tea Parties for their representatives, and exercising their freedom of speech.

The mass media does not show these meetings, or if they do, they portray them as angry mobs. They want to show that people do not support these concerned citizens, but that they support the government. They want them to close their eyes, and that's why they're trying to place blame that you're not as rich or as safe as you could be.

This way, you'll be angry at someone, and people don't think far enough ahead to see that this will destroy opportunities for all. How will it help you? This is the question. Suppose they do what they're saying is right –taking control over the banks, deciding who will receive loans. Suppose they took over automobile companies, and tell you what car you should drive. With any government health care program, with or without the public option, most insurance companies will lose in competition to the government, because government doesn't look at the prices. The insurance companies need to make a profit to survive, because they're a private company. Nobody gives them money.

Then, what happens to you personally? You have to drive a car the government told you to drive; you may or may not get loans because you may or may not fit the government criteria that they told banks to use. And then, if you get sick and you need medication or surgery, and the government says that you're not supposed to have the treatment, there is nowhere for you to go. You're stuck. Right now, if one insurance company says that you cannot get a treatment, you can change your insurance company, or pay for the treatment and medication you want. If the government controls everything and dictates what you can do, you're stuck. There is nowhere for you to maneuver. You're stuck. So, it's one step beyond the anger, and then what?

The definition of progress is to advance and move forward. When I look at the aspirations of American Progressives, I see nothing new or forward-looking. Instead, I see the same ideas that formed the basis of the USSR, which eventually suffered a complete economic collapse.

The Soviet government controlled every aspect of society. Every worker received a salary unrelated to their work; it was closer to welfare, and covered only the necessities. Medicine and education was free and provided by the state, as no one could pay for it. The Soviet economic structure resulted in low productivity, stagnation, outdated technology, and the suppression of creativity and individual initiative.

Today, Progressives want to regulate the salaries of private businesses, and control major industries, banks, and medicine. Especially ironic is that U.S. congressmen—most of whom are lawyers—want to dictate what procedures and medications doctors can provide, and what fees they can charge. Is there any chance that this will improve the quality of medical care? Will this really stimulate the brightest people to go into the medical field?

There is strong pressure by the Progressives to eliminate the secret ballot for union membership. It's called the Employee Free Choice Act, but it's really a card check. It's anything but free. It would be another step backwards to what it was like in the USSR, where all workers were unionized by force – and another way for the state to control its citizens.

The Soviet government confiscated all private property in the name of the collective good. The U.S. Supreme Court case of *Kelo v. City of New London* seems like a first step in this direction. It allowed the transfer of residential private property without their consent to a private developer for the "greater economic good of the municipality." The decision was 5-4, with the progressive justices in the majority.

After the Socialist Revolution in Russia there was a full-blown assault on religion. All public religious symbols were eliminated. The state enforcement of atheist views made it impossible to openly practice any religion.

In the United States, the Constitution protects the separation between church and state. Progressives perverted this ideal to allow atheist zealots to force out religious symbols and traditions from the public space. It is fashionable in the progressive circles to ridicule religion and religious people. *Tolerance* is applied only to anti-religious values.

Progressives tend to view people not as unique individuals, but as groups of people (African-American, white, gay, Hispanic, female, etc.). This is similar to how society was structured by the Soviet government, which saw people in terms of their ethnicity (Ethnic Russian, Jewish, Asian, etc.). This is a dangerous trend for any society, because it is easy for the government to distract people from its own failures by drawing attention to and exploiting ethnic tensions.

It is trendy in America today for popular figures to preach to schoolchildren to serve the "dear president." This is reminiscent of the USSR, where the first thing one saw upon entering any school was the portrait of Lenin, the leader of the Socialist Revolution. On top of the portrait was Lenin's admonition to every child: *"You have to study, study, study – this is your main task."* It seems very well intended – the big and caring Papa wants you to study, but it reminded the children there was a higher authority than their parents and teachers. In the fifth grade, the story of Pavlik Morozov – the "young pioneer"—was required reading. Pavlik reported his father to the secret police. His life exemplified the duty of all good Soviet citizens to serve their government.

"Service" and "sacrifice" are part of the American Progressive lexicon. Sacrifice for what? And to whom? Why is sacrifice to the state considered progressive? Is the Progressive movement driven by ignorance of modern-day history? Or is it the naïve belief that they can better implement the identical policies that failed everywhere else?

I wrote these articles because I wanted to bring attention to what I'm seeing. I hope people will hear the reasons, what's happening –what may happen if these steps actually occur. I hope that in 2010, more people vote against Progressives.

People don't understand that if you tax somebody less, they have more money to put towards everything else, and everybody does better. If you want to pay more taxes, you can write them a check. There aren't enough checks to cover the bureaucracy that the government creates. The inefficiencies of government are stupendous.

On one hand, Obama campaigned like a socialist, and on the other, he drew in people from the center right by saying he'd lower taxes and spending. It seems like it's turning into a real battle of wills by the statist versus the individual.

At one point, I was very pessimistic. But my nature is optimistic. I cannot believe that people who live in a free society like America can be repressed. I don't think 2010 is too late. It will be the most important election in American history. If the Republicans and moderate and conservative Democrats do not succeed in stopping everything Obama and Pelosi are trying to do, America will decline economically and spiritually, and it will lose its power. Russia and China are not friends to America. Their goal has always been to overpower America.

I think the reason so many American people do not appreciate their country's values is because they are not taught in school the modern history of countries around the world and the history of this uniquely humane country.

IBD Exclusive Series:

The Perspective Of A Russian Immigrant

By Svetlana Kunin

IN THE UNION OF Soviet Socialist Republics, I was taught to believe individual pursuits are selfish and sacrificing for the collective good is noble.

In kindergarten we sang songs about Lenin, the leader of the Socialist Revolution. In school we learned about the beautiful socialist system, where everybody is equal and everything is fair; about ugly capitalism, where people are exploited and treat each other like wolves in the wilderness.

Life in the USSR modeled the socialist ideal. God-based religion was suppressed and replaced with cultlike adoration for political figures.

The government-assigned salary of the proletariat (blue-collar worker) was 30%-50% higher than any professional. Without incentive to improve their life, professionals drank themselves to oblivion. They – engineers, lawyers, doctors, teachers – earned a government-determined salary that barely covered the necessities, mainly food.

Raising children was a hardship. It took four to six adults (parents and grandparents) to support a child. The usual size of the postwar family was one or two children. Every woman had the right to have an abortion and most of them did, often without anesthesia.

There is a comparative historical reality that plays out the consequences of two competing ideologies: life in the USSR and in America.

When the march to the worker's paradise — the Socialist Revolution – began in 1917, many people emigrated from Russia to the U.S.

In the USSR, economic equality was achieved by redistributing wealth, ensuring that everyone remained poor, with the exception of those doing the redistributing. Only the ruling class of Communist leaders had access to special stores, medicine and accommodations that could compare to those in the West.

The rest of the citizenry had to deal with permanent shortages of food and other necessities, and had access to free but inferior, unsanitary, and low-tech medical care. The egalitarian utopia of equality, achieved by the sacrifice of individual self-interest for the collective good, led to corruption, black markets, anger, and envy.

Government-controlled health care destroyed human dignity.

Chairman Nikita Khrushchev released facts about Stalin and his purges. People learned of the horrific purge of more than 20 million citizens, murdered as enemies of the state.

Those who left Russia found a different set of values in America: freedom of religion, speech, individual pursuits, the right to private property, and free enterprise. The majority of those immigrants achieved a better life for themselves and their children in this capitalist land.

These opportunities let the average immigrant live a better life than many elites in the Soviet Communist Party. The freedom to pursue personal self-interest led to prosperity. Prosperity generated charity, benefiting the collective good.

The descendants of those immigrants are now supporting policies that move America away from the values that gave so many immigrants the chance of a better life. Policies such as nationalized medicine, high tax rates, and government intrusion into free enterprise are being sold to us under the socialistic motto of collective salvation.

Socialism has bankrupted and failed every society, while capitalism has lifted more people out of poverty than any other system.

There is no perfect society. There are no perfect people. Critics say that greed is the driving force of capitalism. My answer is that envy is the driving force of socialism. Change to socialism is not an improvement on the imperfections of the current system.

The slogans of "fairness and equality" sound better than the slogans of capitalism. But unlike at the beginning of the 20th century, when these slogans and ideas were yet to be tested, we have accumulated history and reality.

Today we can define the better system not by slogans, but by looking at the accumulated facts. We can compare which ideology leads to the most oppression and which brings the most opportunity.

When I came to America in 1980 and experienced life in this country, I thought it was fortunate that those living in the

USSR did not know how unfortunate they were.

Now in 2009, I realize how unfortunate it is that many Americans do not understand how fortunate they are. They vote to give government more and more power without understanding the consequences.

Svetlana Kunin at home in Connecticut, 2009.
(Photos: Courtesy Svetlana Kunin)

Two

POLAND

"We didn't have a normal life under Communism. Our lives were dominated by alcohol and hunting for stuff in the stores... basic, basic things. There was no spiritual part of our lives."

*Agnieszka Bernstein with her mother
in their Lodz neighborhood, 1973*

Poland

ARCHEOLOGICAL EVIDENCE INDICATES that Poland had human habitation since before 4000 BC, but recorded history is sparse before the 9th century. The Polish monarchy withstood various assaults and shifting alliances from the 10th through the mid-18th centuries, including assaults from the Mongols, the Ottoman army, and the Cossacks. After a twenty-five-year war ending in 1582, Russia ceded Lithuania and Estonia to Poland.

In 1587, elections were introduced to determine who would be the Polish king; the Polish monarchy system of government existed until the mid-18th century. In 1791, a new constitution was adopted, drawing heavily upon the 1788 ratification of the U.S. Constitution. The new Polish Constitution was designed to correct inherent defects in the Polish-Lithuanian Commonwealth, and was considered the world's second modern codified national constitution. It was not recognized by Russia, however, and the Russian army invaded Poland in May of 1792. In January 1797, Prussian and Austrian officials met in St. Petersburg, and were signatories to an act that abolished the Polish-Lithuanian state.

In November 1806, France came to Poland's defense when forces commanded by Marshall Joachim Murat entered Warsaw. The following February, Napoleon's army attacked Russian forces at Eylau, Poland. Later that year, the city of Danzig (Gdansk) was blessed with six years of formal independence due to Napoleon's victories. This ended in 1813, when Czar Alexander invaded Warsaw and Prussian forces captured Danzig.

Poland remained under Russian rule throughout the 1800s, although sporadic battles for independence were fought by Polish and Lithuanian revolutionaries. Some freedoms were won in this period, including the return of some farms to private ownership, and the right to speak Polish again. When World War I hostilities broke out in 1914, however, Poland was once again a war-torn nation on the front lines of the Austro-German conflict with Russia. The March 1918 Treaty of Brest-Litovsk ended Russia's involvement in the war, and called for the establishment of five independent countries: Estonia, Latvia, Lithuania, Poland, and Ukraine. However, this treaty was annulled by the armistice signed later that year in November.

The Treaty of Versailles was adopted in June 1919, ending military actions against Germany. The United States never ratified the Treaty of Versailles, and thus never joined the League of Nations despite President Woodrow Wilson's role in its formation. In January 1920, the League of Nations was created, and the city of Danzig became free once again. A 150 million dollar U.S. loan to Poland, Austria, and Armenia was approved to help fund the battle against advancing Russian Communists. In March, the Bolsheviks launched a major offensive against Poland.

In 1922, Lithuania and Poland formally separated, and the Vilnius area was transferred to Lithuanian control. This separation between Poland and Lithuania lasted until April 1923, when Poland annexed central Lithuania, followed by the 1933 Polish occupation of Danzig. Two years later, 60 percent of the voters in Danzig voted for Nazism.

In September of 1938, the Munich Agreement was signed by British, Italian, French, and German leaders in an attempt to appease Adolf Hitler. Czechoslovakia's Sudetenland, occupied by a German minority, was given to Germany. The Teschen area was given to Poland, and parts of Slovakia were turned over to Hungary. After signing this agreement, British Prime Minister Neville Chamberlain declared "peace for our time." In November, Poland signed a non-aggression pact with Russia to guard against a German invasion. In March 1939, Germany demanded to be given Danzig, even though Hitler claimed the German-Polish non-attack treaty was still valid. In May, Hitler expressed the desire to occupy Poland. On September 9th, the German army invaded Warsaw.

During the last three months of 1939, Poland and Lithuania were carved up and divided between Germany and the new Soviet Union. The Holocaust began in earnest, with the extermination, forced labor, or exportation of Polish Jews to concentration camps such as Auschwitz in German-occupied Poland.

In early March 1940, Stalin signed an order for the massacre of 21,768 Polish military officers, priests, and other "intellectuals" taken prisoner during the invasion. In April and May, another 25,700 Polish citizens were executed by the NKVD, the Soviet Secret Police, in the towns of Katyn and Miednoje in what is now Ukraine. The Jewish ghetto of Lodz was sealed off by the Germans with barbed wire, and in October the Warsaw ghetto was created, with an October 31st deadline for more than 450,000 Jews to occupy seventy-five square blocks.

In October 1941, construction began on a new concentration camp named Birkenau, a mile and a half from Auschwitz. In December, another camp called Chelmno opened in occupied Poland, designed specifically for the extermination of prisoners. In March 1942, the Belzac concentration camp opened, quickly followed by even more camps such as Treblinka, Sobibor, Majdanek, Stutthof, and *Kraków-Plaszów*. When the Red Army arrived at Auschwitz and Birkenau in January 1945, the death toll was estimated to be 15,000 Soviet POWs, 21,000 Gypsies, 75,000 Polish Christians, and over one million Jews.

In August of 1945, the Communist-dominated Polish government signed a treaty with the Soviet Union and ceded its eastern lands, putting them under Soviet control. The Allies settled on the Oder-Neisse line as the new western Polish border, and the former German city of Breslau was ceded to Poland and renamed Wroclaw. Near the end of 1949, Poland confirmed its adherence to Soviet policy, and in 1950 the Polish government confiscated the property of the Polish church. The Polish Catholic church signed an accord with the government, but still forfeited its principal charitable organization, Caritas.

A new Polish constitution was adopted in 1952, and in May 1955 the Warsaw Pact was signed by the countries of the Soviet bloc: Albania, Bulgaria, Czechoslovakia, East Germany (the Communist German Democratic Republic), Hungary, Poland, Romania, and the Soviet Union. In June, the Soviet Union dispatched tanks to Pozan, Poland, to put down anti-Communist demonstrations.

In early 1968, students took to Warsaw streets protesting Polish government repression, with the chant "Down with the dictatorship!" In August, a conference was held in Bratislava, Slovakia, to consider Czechoslovakia's right to self-determination. Attendees were East Germany, Poland, Hungary, the Soviet Union, and Czechoslovakia. Although the resulting statement confirmed Czechoslovakia's right to pursue its own destiny, the country was invaded on August 20th by 650,000 Soviet bloc troops to crush the "Prague Spring" liberalization of the Alexander Dubček administration.

In December 1970, Poland's General Wojciech Jaruzelski imposed martial law upon the country, but riots continued throughout the month as Poles took to the streets protesting higher food prices. Sixty-four people were killed as tanks and troops brutally restored order in the streets.

In mid-August of 1980, some seventeen thousand Polish workers were organized by Lech Walesa and struck the Lenin Shipyards in Gdansk for seventeen days. This was the birth of Poland's Solidarity (*Solidarność*) labor movement. In September, the movement was formalized with delegates from thirty-six trade unions. In November, eighteen Communist Party secretaries were ousted from Polish provinces, and in December NATO warned the Soviets to stay out of Polish internal affairs. The labor movement spread to private farmers as well, under the name of Rural Solidarity. In January 1981, Walesa won an accord giving workers Saturdays off.

On October 18, 1981, General Jaruzelski was elected party leader, and on December 12th he imposed martial law on Poland. Four days later, riot police fired upon miners protesting in Katowice, with nine killed and twenty-five wounded. Lech Walesa was arrested, and on December 22nd, Polish ambassadors Zdzislaw Rurarz and Romuald Spasowski, defected to the United States in protest of martial law. On the 29th, President Ronald Reagan stopped trade with the Soviet Union as reprisal for these harsh social policies.

In October of 1982, all Polish labor and trade unions were banned. However, Lech Walesa was released from prison on November 11th and martial law was scheduled for termination on July 22, 1983. Lech Walesa was named winner of the Nobel Peace Prize on October 5th, and the U.S. Medal of Freedom in November. In April of 1989, the Solidarity movement was legalized after a seven-year government ban, and the first free elections in forty years were held on June 4th. In January 1990, the Communist Polish Workers Party was dissolved as the country began its transition to democracy. Lech Walesa was elected president of Poland in December.

In 1992, the left-wing populist party Samoobrona was created in Poland as a small farmers' movement. On September 19, 1993, Polish voters gave the most parliamentary seats to the Democratic Left Alliance, followed by the narrow November 1995 win of former Communist Alexander Kwaśniewski over President Lech Walesa. On May 13, 1997, Poland underwent a pension crisis where a full one-fifth of the GDP was being used for pensions and social security. On May 25th, a new constitution was adopted, replacing the 1952 Communist-era charter, with commitments to a market economy, private ownership, personal freedoms, and civilian control of the military.

On September 23, 2001, the Democratic Left Alliance won with 41 percent of the popular vote. Former Communist Leszek Miller became the new Prime Minister. In early 2003, the year-old left-leaning government under Miller collapsed after an emergency meeting between coalition partners. Negotiations broke down in a bitter dispute sparked by a new tax plan. On March 26, 2004, Miller announced his plans to step down the day after Poland planned entry into the European Union on May 1. Twenty-two members of Miller's SLD party had previously left to create the new left-wing Polish Social Democracy party as Miller's popularity plummeted.

Agnieszka Bernstein

*"It wasn't equal opportunity – it was enforced
equal outcome. There was no chance of success."*

I WAS BORN IN 1973 in Lodz, which is the second biggest city in Poland, right in the middle of the country. Politically, the country was really entrenched in Communism. My first memories growing up were of living in a very small, one-bedroom apartment, with my parents, grandparents, uncle, older brother, and our dog. It was very crowded. In the cities, almost everyone lived in public housing. It was extremely rare for people to live in private homes or apartments in the cities, but it was different in the country.

Our apartment building looked like the projects here in America, but they weren't dangerous and crime-ridden. There was some drug activity, but people didn't have guns. They were just very poor. There were a lot of thugs, and it was common to get mugged or raped in the street. If people died from shootings, we never heard about it because we had no free press. When I was seven, we moved to a better government apartment, really luxurious by Polish standards. By American standards, it was really mediocre.

My grandparents were very simple, uneducated people from the country who used to be farmers. My grandmother was taken as one of the slaves to Germany as a little girl. Her entire childhood was interrupted by the war. When the Germans invaded Poland, they made it all the way to Lodz in 1939. The Germans had no regard for the Poles, and many people who survived were loaded in trains and shipped to Germany as slave labor. She was one of them.

When the war ended in 1945, she walked all the way back to Poland from Germany – many people did that. It took weeks to walk back home. My great-grandmother dressed all the girls up as boys and covered them up to escape rape by the Russian soldiers.

My grandmother made needles in a factory for the Communist Party. The leadership's goal was to have as many people as possible join the Party. My grandparents were both religious, and the Church campaigned very strongly against Party membership. I'm personally not very religious, but I think the church in Poland, especially John Paul II, had an incredible role in breaking Communism. It cannot be underestimated – it was just tremendous.

For centuries, the Church held the power of kings in check, and now it was the Communists. The Communist Party was the only entity in the government, and if it weren't for the Church, people would not have any other place to turn. It was like a state within a state, and it was a very popular counterbalance against the Communist Party.

My grandparents were pretty religious, uneducated, simple people from the country. They never wanted to join the Communist Party, and that's one of the things that my grandfather was very proud of. They always tried to sign him up, and he always said no – the Communist Party members frequently approached him at work. He thinks he could have gotten a better salary and more holidays if he joined the Party. There were definitely carrots there, but both he and my father didn't want to do that.

May first in Poland was Labor Day. It was a huge Communist holiday, and everyone gathered and waved big red flags. Many people don't know that it wasn't voluntary. To get a big turnout, they gave free vodka to the workers as a political tool. Even my grandfather, who wouldn't join the Communist Party, went because he got free vodka. He even carried that red flag, even though he didn't believe in it.

My grandmother told me the factory she worked in made needles for export to the West. That was very unusual, so it was a good factory. She worked on a piecework basis, and was paid according to how many needles she made. She tried hard to work fast, and to make them well. But if she exceeded the limit after which she would be paid more, they changed the limit. After a few years of this, she just didn't care anymore. Why should she work hard? She thought they just liked screwing with her head. They often did things like that to discourage people, because they didn't have the money to pay them anyway.

Poland also produced vodka for export – that was how the country got hard money. Many families had alcohol problems in Poland back then. For me, one of the most important things that happened with the fall of Communism was liberating Polish people from alcohol addiction. And now, when I talk to my old friends from Poland, I am discovering that their parents had alcohol problems, too. I never knew that because my own father had an alcohol problem. But of course, it was something you'd hide, and you didn't want anybody else to know about it. I never had my friends over, because I was afraid that he'd be drunk when I came home. But now I find out that it wasn't just me. We didn't have any possibilities for anything better, and my whole childhood, I dealt with my father's drinking.

I was a teenager when the Berlin Wall fell in 1989, and when the Communist system crumbled, it healed my father. When we were growing up, he worked in a state-owned bakery in a hotel. The restaurant and the bakery always had a lot of alcohol around, and because people weren't paid by merit, they did whatever they wanted. I remember my father went on and off the wagon for most of my childhood: drunk for weeks, and then sober for weeks.

All that changed in 1989, when all the big state companies were privatized. My father's company was a big conglomerate, and he got an offer to buy out the bakery that he worked for. My parents went back and forth about it. It was a big decision, because we didn't know anything other than being told what to do. Back then, we didn't know anything about accounting, ordering, selling – it was a huge task.

My father said, okay, let's try, let's do it. He had to buy a car. When I was growing up, it was the biggest dream – a car?! Are you kidding me? That was so luxurious, and I never, ever thought we'd have a car. He had to buy a car, and had to become responsible. He was actually a very good baker. He had to hire people, and he had to become responsible for himself. That's when he stopped drinking.

With the change from Communism to a free market, it truly changed our lives. It wasn't the money – it was my father taking responsibility for himself. I didn't really have to be worried again. That was one of the most important changes in my life: The fall of Communism healed my dad from his drinking addiction.

My mom had been a gym teacher, and a few years into running the bakery in the free market economy, she quit her job and started working with him. He's since passed away, but they were very successful and they have a beautiful, modern home. My brother, who was working with her, does, too. They employ around thirty workers now. It's been an incredible change over there.

When we lived under Communism, the stores were always empty. All the shelves in the grocery store were empty, except maybe rows of vinegar, just for display. The drugstore shelves were either empty or filled up with only one product, like cleanser. There were shortages all the time. If there was a delivery of any kind to a store; there was always a line – always. It was a rule. If there was no line in front of a store, don't even go there, because there's nothing there.

I particularly hated it as a little kid, because my mom used me to get in line. There was a law that mothers with children under a certain age had a right to cut in line. For a long time, she told people I was smaller than I was. I'd whine, "No! I'm more than five!" and she had to *shush* me. When I was too big for her to carry me, I had to wait around with her, usually three or four hours. She'd get off work, and then go straight to the store and wait in line till the evening.

We did this day after day. We didn't have a normal life under Communism. Our lives were dominated by alcohol and hunting for stuff in the stores... basic, basic things. There was no spiritual part of our lives. Americans often despair that they're so materialistic. Actually, *we* were the materialistic ones; we became very animal-like, because we were deprived of material goods. We had no time for the luxury of spirituality. It was just subsistence survival.

People say that when you meet Eastern Europeans, they can seem kind of rude or they lack social skills – it's because of what we went through. Even now, I sometimes tell my mom, "It's okay. Nobody's going to push you out of the way."

It's this ingrained animal instinct for survival, only focusing on what you have to get.

We waited in lines my entire childhood. Always in line, always in line. And then in 1981, Solidarity started causing trouble for the Communists. The government imposed martial law, with many new rules restricting what liberty we used to have. We weren't allowed on the street at all after six p.m. until about eight in the morning. But you still had to go out and get your food.

I remember one Christmas, my mother had to get some food in the morning, but it was still before eight o'clock. She went downstairs in our apartment building, and hid in the lobby. There was already a line of people in front of the store, waiting for it to open. She was really torn: "Should I go? Should I not go? But it's too early. Oh, my God, there's going to be a line. Should I risk it?" She didn't risk it, and decided to wait. It was a good decision, because at two minutes till eight, the police rolled in and put everybody in the vans. The police drove the vans around for several hours and then let everybody out in the middle of nowhere. They had to find their own way back home. They wouldn't bring you to prison, but it did make your life difficult.

Funny, this was the best Christmas ever because my mom was the first customer in the store. Everybody else had been arrested, and she was able to buy lots of good food for us!

Another time we went into a store, and the only thing in the store was pepper! So we bought pepper – a lot of it. I knew my mom was hoarding pepper – everybody did that because they were so deprived. We had two drawers full of pepper.

When my father passed away, my grandmother moved in with my mom. When we helped her move and opened her armoire, it was just stuffed with things from the Communist era: fabrics and clothes that still had the old Communist tags on it, because she'd never used them. She never needed it, but she was just hoarding them, just in case. Almost thirty years later, and she's still hoarding stuff.

There was an active underground exchange market, especially between the city and the country people. Sadly, farmers were not allowed to sell to private people, and they had to sell to the government for a set price, which is, of course, very low. Farmers sold their crops on the black market to people, but it was really pretty dangerous. Once we visited my family in the country, and we bartered with our uncle for a pig so we could make our own sausages. We were stopped by the police on the way home, and they just checked our papers. My father was terrified, because, oh my God, we had this pig in the trunk. At minimum, they would take it from us. But we probably could have been in trouble, and my uncle could have gotten in trouble, too.

There was a lot of illegal, black market barter. You go the doctor, and you don't give them money. Money couldn't buy you anything. Money was worthless. It was just a piece of paper, really, because you go to the store, and there's nothing there. So, when you go to the doctor, you always have to bring something with you. Health care is a whole other story. It was so corrupt.

Even today, my aunt tries to pay the doctor in the hospital – once she tried to give him three thousand dollars! I tell her, "You can't do it, that's over. They get paid. You can't give them money." These are old habits. In Poland, if you didn't pay them, the doctors just wouldn't take care of you.

Health care was free, and doctors would make house calls, which we used a lot, of course. The doctor would treat you just okay, but as soon as you gave him something extra, suddenly there would be a prescription for some real medicine, and the doctor became a different person. It corrupted doctors tremendously. My sister had a serious condition, and she couldn't get the referral for a specialist until she bribed the doctor.

You had to know who to pay off, and very often, the doctor in charge of the hospital would take bribes, big time. You wouldn't pay him directly, but you'd give it to a friend of a friend who knows a friend, and suddenly, a hospital bed became available. It was really serious stuff.

Dental care was free, too, but you couldn't choose. Private practices were against the law – everything had to be public. So that way, rich people didn't get better treatment than poor people. Right. You couldn't get toothpaste or even a toothbrush! I remember brushing with my *finger!* We used tooth powder for a long time, gritty stuff that you mixed with water. We even got free dental care in school, but what they *don't* tell you is the dentists were very rough, and the equipment wasn't up to date. All the dentists were really kind of tired, and they were resentful that they had to serve all those people. I think they felt like machines.

I've had my teeth drilled without any shots or medication. I've spent so much money on my teeth since I've been in the United States. If something was wrong, the dentist just pulled your tooth out, because they didn't have the right materials to treat you. When you look at Eastern Europeans, their teeth are pretty messed up. An American smile is very famous in Europe. When someone in Eastern Europe smiles, half their teeth are gone.

For some reason, the Communists allowed us a peek at American culture once in a while. Every Sunday, they showed us American movies or cartoons as a special treat. They knew they were better. Sometimes they showed Rocky or Rambo. How stupid was that? Rocky and Rambo were our biggest heroes – we loved them. I'm not star-struck, and I hate the celebrity thing, but if I could ever meet someone, it would be Sylvester Stallone.

There were government-owned stores in Poland that were only for foreigners. You could only use hard cash – dollars or other Western currency. I think you could bribe them to sell you something, but you had to show a passport proving you were a foreigner. I remember looking at all this stuff as a kid, like the Gummi Bears. Everything was so colorful and beautiful, but it was out of reach for us, of course.

Our apartment complex had a huge parking lot, but there were only a couple of cars in it. One was owned by the janitor, who was in the Communist Party, and one was owned by my father's friend, who was trading currency illegally. He did that right in front of the bank, and people hoarded dollars because the inflation was just crazy. Every day, prices went up. When you hear about German hyperinflation in 1920s, using wheelbarrows full of money to pay for a loaf of bread... that's what happened in Poland.

All the savings were in dollars or Deutschemarks, and selling or trading Western currency was illegal. I think the traders were also police informants; otherwise they wouldn't be allowed to hang out on the street corners trading cash.

Survival was the primary concern for people. For people to think of political change or protest – it was too much. Everybody was very scared. I remember my uncle listened to Radio Free Europe – it was a very big thing in Poland, and it was forbidden. You were not allowed to tell anybody you listened.

I have a friend whose father from Poland had been imprisoned. He was active with Solidarity, and they fled to Sweden because they were afraid for their lives. But politically, for simple people like us, there was no room for thinking about protesting when we needed to survive just day to day.

If you have to wait in line three hours a day, every day, where do you get the energy? At some point, the economy was really bad; it was somewhat connected to some dissent within the Polish government with Russia. The Russians controlled all the energy going into Poland, and even today, they use Russian gas. Our energy was rationed, meaning that in the summer, there was never any hot water. They just didn't heat it up. And often, there was no electricity for some reason. I'm not sure if it was they were so screwed up, they couldn't run the plant, or if they were saving money, but very often, we had blackouts for a few hours, usually in the evening and overnight.

At school, we had huge holes in history that we never touched. There was an atrocity during World War II when Stalin's secret police executed over 21,000 Polish officers. They took them to the Katyn Forest and executed them all. We never learned about that, and we were never taught where the actual border of Poland was before the war.

It was interesting how isolated we were. Surprisingly, we didn't trade with other Eastern European countries, China, or any other Communist countries at all. It was like North Korea – it was very strange that way. The whole campaign was for us to buy Polish, be patriotic. We were very isolated from everybody else. Maybe we didn't trade with other Communist countries because the production was in shambles. The quality of the goods were so shoddy that they were virtually worthless in trade with even other Communist countries.

When you grow up in Communism, you have to learn how to do every single thing from scratch, because you just can't buy anything that's worth anything. You'd either have to make your own clothes, or fix whatever they sell you. A pair of pants would have different length legs, and new garments had holes in them – there was no quality control. There was an expression in Poland: you sleep or you work, you get the same pay. It was true.

Lech Walesa and the labor unions started the Solidarity movement in 1980 to protest Soviet Communism, and there were little fire points all over the country. The government imposed a curfew, and then martial law in 1981 – it was very repressive. After a couple of years, they had to negotiate with Solidarity, and made a deal to give them a little bit of freedom, a little more pay. By 1989, the government had lost and Walesa was elected president of Poland. There was so much poverty and inefficiency that they probably didn't even care anymore. There was nothing left in Poland or Russia, nothing left to fight for... or exploit.

The Church has had a tremendous role in Poland. There was one very outspoken priest who was eventually imprisoned and killed by the Communists. He spoke out during mass against the government, and told the people what to do. It was brave. He probably knew what was going to happen. Even though he suffered for it, his words were heard. Lots of priests played a very positive role.

I came to the United States in December 2001. I went to college in Poland and had a little multimedia company with my boyfriend. It was okay to travel, and we'd come here for trade shows and other business. America was the biggest, most wonderful dream, like Ayn Rand thought. I have to mention her because she's a very big influence on me. I eventually broke up with my boyfriend; I met my husband, we got married, and I just stayed.

Poland is very pro-America – that's why we sent troops to Iraq. America is far enough away to be exciting, but we especially remember Ronald Reagan, for what he did to help us.

The Communist government fed us all kinds of crazy stories. For example, we had a potato bug infestation. When we went to the movies, they showed Communist propaganda before the actual movie. They told us that the Americans dropped the potato bugs out of planes because they were imperialistic swine who hated how wonderful and rich life was in our socialist heaven. That's what they told us, seriously. They actually called it the American bug! Once someone tells you so many bad things about something, at some point, you start thinking, hey, it might be this way.

I didn't know that Ayn Rand even existed for a very long time. A friend of mine suggested I read her books; that surprised me because I always thought he was ultra-liberal. It just hit me – *boom!* Nothing ever influenced me in my life as much as *Atlas Shrugged*. It was great timing, because it was right before all the bailouts happened in 2008. I wish people knew more about the book and the philosophy around it. I'm going to art school, and my goal is to draw a graphic novel based on it. I went to school because of that. It's a never-ending influence, the whole philosophy. Graphic novels are experiencing a rebirth, and I think this would be a great way to promote Ayn Rand's morality and ideas. It's a huge project, and maybe I'll also do a parody of my childhood under Communism.

When I first came to the U.S., I had very little savings, and I worked in a coffee shop. After I met my husband, I worked for another year, and then really took it easy. I'd wake up late because I really didn't have to get up. Then it was too late to really accomplish anything. I can see why people who are on welfare don't have any motivation to do anything with their lives. I think it's hurting them tremendously. Even though they're poor now, they can still have a goal in life. That's where *real* self-esteem comes from – from doing something difficult and achieving it. And you go, yeah, I did that! And I can do it again!

I think President Obama's been a very polarizing figure, and he's made everybody angry enough that they're now motivated. People on the far left don't like him because he hasn't delivered the socialist utopia, and of course, people who are moderate and to the right can't stand him, either, because he's pushing a big government, socialist agenda.

My husband is Jewish, and they tend to vote Democrat; he actually voted for Obama. He's registered Democrat, but he's a true independent. He's very disappointed. He thought Obama said all those things to get more people to vote for him, but he thought, there's no way he's going to do all this crazy stuff. Now, when I ask him if he's going to vote for him again, he says no, he's not.

The statism I see in the administration now is reminiscent of what I left in Poland... and it's not even taking over the auto companies or banks. It's the state implanting the idea in people's heads that you have to live for the state... sacrificing yourself for the greater good. He's pandering to the younger people. It's scary: the entitlements, the whole mentality. You can do great things for society without sacrificing your personal liberties. When you're the most productive, you're the most creative, and you're always raising the bar. There's nothing moral about enabling people to do nothing, and just depending on others to survive.

When I hear debate, sadly, politicians don't use the moral case. They say it's practical, that it works better, or it doesn't work – but they don't make the moral case. And ultimately, I think until you do that, they're going to lose the battle.

I believe that for our country to change direction and get back on track, we have to stop this sanction of the victim. For me personally, I'd like to reach people with graphic novels that promote self-reliance and objectivism. It's important for people to speak out. At the Tax Day Tea Party in 2009, I had a big sign that read, "I Heart Capitalism." It's important to write letters to the editor to support whatever cause you believe in – the left does it. We have to do it, too.

Recently, there was a Von Mises conference here in San Francisco – it was a very white crowd. We need to engage minorities in the process: the Asian community, the Indian community, Latinos, black people, young people, everybody. Liberty is for everyone.

In Poland, things got so hard that people starting doing something and Solidarity started. On the other hand, if it had been up to farmers and factory workers, it never would have been organized. But Walesa was the face of it, and he had the Polish people behind him.

It's the nature of young people to rebel. The administration is pushing the socialist/statist agenda down our throats so fast, I think they'll overreach to the point where the young people will rebel. I don't think they'll go for the Internet being controlled by the government or having their tweets screened.

Obama says he'll give tax cuts to welfare recipients, people who don't pay any taxes. I think businessmen have to stand up for themselves; they have to speak out. They can't keep on apologizing for their success, feeling guilty for it. I think accomplishing to the fullest is one of the most moral things you can do. A poor person never gave me a job!

Also, I think the multiculturalism that's taking over the world is a very dangerous concept. I really resent that. It's like knocking down a whole building so somebody else can come in and put their building on our land. It really hurts the quality of teaching, telling people not to use your judgment at all. You need to be judgmental to survive –using your judgment is not the same thing being cruel. You even use your judgment when looking at art.

In Russia, they used to have a very strict rule about what you could paint and what you could not. But they were trained really well, and they started young. They were very talented, but again, they were very restricted in what they could paint. These artists grew up in this culture of painting farmers and workers, and how great Communism was. But they developed an underground movement of painting what they wanted. They discovered what was going on in the West, even though they're a little behind the times.

As an artist who grew up in Communist Poland, when I saw the Obama campaign posters, the first thing I thought was, it's Communism. It's the same stuff, the same style. I never thought I would see that in America. I grew up in that; people who didn't live it have this idealistic idea about sharing with other people. It's immoral in some ways, because in Poland, people were coerced to do that. How can people think socialism is great?

I remember the *Newsweek* cover with the red and blue handshake in the Communist block art that said, "We are all socialists now." I stopped buying *Newsweek* after that. Even after the inauguration, Obama kept giving campaign speeches, but there was nothing specific about his plans. In Poland, Party members didn't have to be specific or explain themselves. There was always a plan: We had a two-year plan, a three-year plan, a five-year plan, and when one plan ended, there was always another one. There were just a lot of speeches, no follow-through, no accountability after the plan was over. They say things that are kind of vague, and then you fill in the blanks of whatever you want to hear. I think that's just what happened during Obama's campaign.

I hope that people will wake up before it gets really bad. Things are going so fast. For me, the biggest thing about the end of Communism was my father taking responsibility for his life. That was the most tremendous change, and that happened in many other people's lives, too.

Growing up in Poland, everybody lived in the projects, and everybody was the same – but it brought everybody down to the lowest level. You could be a janitor, a doctor, grandmother, teacher, factory worker, all living together, all being identical. It really hurt people who were hard working and educated. It wasn't equal opportunity – it was enforced equal outcome. The government tried to make sure that the outcome of everybody's lives was as equal as possible. Nobody was better or more successful than anybody else, but everybody was brought down to the same level of misery. Pretty much all the joy goes out of your life – there was no chance of success.

You had to deal with people in the government, so it's like dealing with the Mafia. Or you could join the Communist Party. My parents never did, but I have an uncle who was pretty successful back then. He had a private restaurant, which was very unusual in Poland. And now, I can't talk to him – he never said straight out when I asked him if he's ever been in the Communist Party or the secret police. He just said, "Well, I've been a member of many organizations."

There are still lots of apparatchiks in Poland now, but now there are modern homes, with no mortgages because people save and pay cash. There are shopping malls and stuff like we have here – it's amazing. It's like a different country. There are even enough cars to have traffic jams.

In the Communist days, we'd take a taxi to visit my grandparents. We waited in line for a taxi for a frickin' half hour. There were gypsy cabs, but it was very dangerous, so there were very few of them. We stood in the cold, with snow coming down, with twenty people in front of you waiting for a taxi, and it was an old, beat-up car with no heat. The pollution was the worst. You think, the government is big, it's going to take care of the environment. It was *awful*. Why would the government force any standards on the factories that they owned? So, the pollution was just terrible.

There's another thing I'm very much against. People talk about all the green regulations, and that we should have a better train system. I believe that cars in America are probably the single most important thing that give you independence. Those transportation unions in France keep the government in check all the time, whenever they want – and they know when to strike, too. They do it on holidays. They can paralyze the whole of France because people have no private means of transportation. Yes, we have traffic jams, but nothing will give you more independence than getting in your own car and driving wherever you want.

So many people are bought off by so little, and with a welfare and entitlement mentality, all it takes is just a regular check every two weeks for somebody to have no ambition, no desire to get up, go out, and *do* something! I know... I lived it. That's what happens to your personality. If your need for survival is removed from you, you become lethargic and lazy. It destroys you.

I love having the Internet and alternative media. That's the best thing to happen to this country. I love it. Especially living in San Francisco, it's so liberal. I was starting to become bitter, but now I've learned to enjoy being a minority. I've really embraced it. I talk to people who are very liberal about Communism – and they always say the same thing: "Oh, it failed because they didn't do it right. We know how to do it right. They made mistakes."

I really think that the heart of the problem is embracing your individual rights, to have a right to live, to make money, to be proud of it, not to apologize for it. You cannot be embarrassed about succeeding. You just cannot do that.

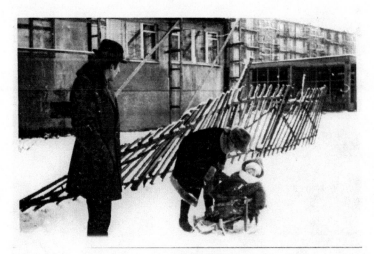

Agnieszka Bernstein with her parents in front
of their Lodz apartment building, mid-1970s.

Agnieszka and her brother on summer vacation, late 1970s.

Agnieszka, her parents and workers at their family bakery, 2006.
(All Photos: Courtesy Agnieszka Bernstein)

Three

ITALY

"Absolutely no meetings of any kind were allowed, other than the Mussolini gatherings for the children, or they were accused of being American spies."

The Arcangeli family, taken 1954 in Rome.
(Photo: Courtesy Anna Arcangeli)

Italy

Born in 1883, Benito Amilcare Andrea Mussolini is widely regarded as the father of modern fascism (*fascio* in Italian). The son of a socialist blacksmith and a teacher, Mussolini learned early in life to always question authority, and was urged constantly by his mother Rosa to never miss an opportunity to change society "for the sake of future generations."

An unusually bright child, Mussolini also earned a reputation as a troublemaker. Like his anticlerical father, he had a disdain for religion, and showed it by pinching members of the congregation at his mother's church, as well as by throwing rocks at them. Mussolini earned a trip to reform school, and was then expelled for stabbing a fellow student and throwing an inkwell at an instructor. No matter, his grades were good enough to eventually earn a post as a school principal.

Mussolini avoided the World War I draft by fleeing to Switzerland, and found work as an editor for the socialist newspaper *Avanti*. He later abandoned socialism and his message became fascism, where he envisioned all power residing properly in the hands of one individual – himself.

In 1921, Mussolini was elected to the Italian parliament, where he organized bands of war veterans – *squadristi* or terror squads – to roam the streets and attack socialists, Communists, and anarchists. Strike-breaking became his specialty, and the industrialists of the time were enormously thankful for the resulting order.

In November 1921, the multiple fascist organizations coalesced into the Fascist Party. Mussolini and his Blackshirts, which originated as his *squadristi*, marched on Rome in October 1922 to establish the primacy of the Fascist Party in Italy. That month, Mussolini announced at a party conference, "Either the government will be given to us, or we shall seize it by marching on Rome." Fascists descended on Rome from all over Italy and occupied the public buildings. Mussolini demanded that a new Fascist government be installed.

After the March on Rome, Italy's King Victor Emmanuel III asked Mussolini to form a new government, and three days later Mussolini became Italy's youngest prime minister at thirty-nine. This was for show, however; the king had asked him to fill that office before the March on Rome even occurred.

His following meteoric rise to power can be attributed to his ability to manipulate the press, the economic uncertainty of the time, and the Italian people's fear of being drawn into another war. Mussolini was the handsome and charismatic leader they craved.

Mussolini's hatred of socialism, Communism, and unionism intensified, and *Il Duce* ("The Leader," as he christened himself) increased his power over the next twenty years. Adolf Hitler studied Mussolini's fascistic successes for a decade before the German people elected him to power.

In 1940, Mussolini agreed with Hitler to align Italy with Germany's fight against France and Britain. The relationship between the two started well, but Hitler eventually tired of Mussolini's constant strutting and preening, and relegated him to a minor role where decisions about the war effort were concerned. Following successive defeats by the Allies, Mussolini was arrested and removed from power in June 1943, and imprisoned in the Alpine retreat of Gran Sasso. He was rescued that September by the Nazi *Fallschirmjäger* paratrooper unit, and taken to a meeting with Hitler, who insisted that the tired and ill Mussolini return to Italy and establish a new fascist state. The resulting Italian Social Republic was a puppet government of the Germans.

When the U.S. 10th Mountain Division finally routed the Nazis from Italy's northern mountains in 1944, it was obvious that Hitler was in no position to extend any further help to Italy's former golden boy dictator. In March 1945, Italy's Communist Party called for an armed uprising. On April 17th, Mussolini fled to Milan. Ten days later, Mussolini and his mistress Claretta Petacci were captured by Italian partisans as the pair attempted to escape to Switzerland in a German convoy. He was hidden in the back of a truck wearing the uniform of the Fascist militia.

Mussolini's past terror squads, from his *squadristi* in the Twenties to the later Blackshirts, were not forgotten by his foes. The partisan leaders, led by the Communists, executed Mussolini, his mistress, and fifteen other fascists on April 29th. Since Mussolini had a habit of hanging the bodies of Communists upside down on meat hooks in the piazza, their bodies were hung upside down from the rafters of a half-built gas station in Milan.

.

Anna Arcangeli

"Get the government out of people's lives.
Socialism wants to control everything."

DURING THE SECOND WORLD WAR, we lived in Rome, right across the street from the Nazi S.S. headquarters. There was an extreme lack of food during the war, so we children took walks right in front of their headquarters, trying to win their approval and the hearts of the S.S. We were hungry, and we wanted to eat. We were trying to befriend the German S.S.

In time, the S.S. softened their hearts towards us. In their free time, they came out to walk and play with us. As we played near them, the S.S. saw that we reminded them of their own children in Germany, and that we were well-mannered. We were very hungry and oppressed, and the S.S. started giving us some of their own food.

Mussolini had been in power for about six years when I was born in 1928. We were starving because my father was taken by the S.S. as a political prisoner. His name was Luigi Arcangeli – the Archangel in Italian. Mama's name was Elvira; she was an Ashkenazi Jew, and she converted to Christianity. Her maiden name was Rocchi, which translates to Stein.

Papa and Mama were respected and loved by the community. Because he was the pastor of the Assemblies of God church, the Germans did not appreciate his religion or the political revolt against them. He was taken to jail, and he was on his way to the concentration camp.

So, we were hungry. We had nothing. The head of our family was gone, so we befriended the Germans, and got some food from them. Unfortunately and unbeknownst to them, the Germans sent a spy as an assistant to an older relative, just to help her out, or so they said. But the spy was reporting to the Germans – that's why Father was arrested.

The schools and the quality of the teaching were very good, but it was rubber-stamped. Everybody was the same. There was no rich, no poor – everybody was the same. Nobody had the opportunity to be original or individual. Everybody had to wear the same uniform.

When I was around eleven, we were required to go to school on Saturdays. They collected children from the neighborhood, whether they were middle-class, rich or not, and they would treat us all the same. We played and marched in the large gym and were indoctrinated by Mussolini's regime. It became a very orderly thing, and we had to wear uniforms. This is how they began the recruitment into the Blackshirt Youth. My age group was called the Little Italians. I had a black pleated skirt, a white blouse with an emblem of Mussolini on the blouse, and a little black hat. That was the uniform we had to wear during the indoctrination.

If you missed a few sessions, they would come looking for you, and they forced you to go back. If a family refused to send their children, it was not looked upon favorably, and they could be in fear for their lives. I knew some parents who refused to let their children be indoctrinated into this program, and did not send them. However, they got away with it because things changed as Mussolini became closer to Hitler. There were more important things to go after at the time, and Mussolini's concentration shifted to different goals. He had achieved what he wanted, and had enough children.

Once, I found a moldy piece of bread on the street. I was tired of going to the park to find pine nuts, opening them up and eating them. When I found the piece of bread, I thought I had found a treasure. I scraped the mold off it and ate it. I got a stomachache from eating it, but to me, it was a great find. We looked for greens we thought we could eat in the fields, but once we took them home, Mother told us they were inedible. We were very disappointed and hungry.

The food shortages began when the Germans blocked the roads coming into Rome, and the trucks could not get in. There were no farms in Rome. There was food rationing everywhere, and the rations became smaller and smaller. In order to get food, each person had to bring their rationing booklet to a food center. They clipped a coupon that said you received that piece of bread, and no more. That was it. Every family had a booklet for each member of the family, and we went for bread every day. When we went home with the bread, Mama weighed it on a scale, and divided it between the seven children. She told us the piece had to last us the whole day. The hunger made us a little crafty.

My mother befriended some of the distributors, and when she got the rations for our family, she didn't give them all of the booklets of coupons – she held back one or two. The people would just clip them off, because it was always the same person coming for the same number of people. They took the coupons, but there were seven, not nine. After she got the nine rations, only seven coupons were clipped. Then she went to a different outlet, brought the other two booklets, and got additional rations.

Sometimes, my mama folded the coupons inward when the booklets were all stacked up, and the clerk didn't cut all of them. We were skinny and hungry, and the rationing by the regime was so severe that we never had enough food.

We had nine people in the family before Papa was taken to prison in 1945. They took his rationing book away. He was released after the war ended. They opened the prisons for the political prisoners – not the violent criminals, just the thieves and murderers. He was a political prisoner because he was a minister, and was captured near the end of the war.

Mussolini was alive when Papa was taken. Papa held a service that Sunday, and my oldest sister Maria took part in an official rowing match on the Tiber River. Many of her teammates were Mussolini youth, but we weren't fascists. After the service, Papa rode his bike to the match, and went home afterwards. The S.S. had stormed his church right after the service and arrested the people inside, but did not catch Papa because he left right away to watch Maria.

After the match, he came home to have dinner with us. The S.S. who arrested the people at church were out looking for Papa, since he was the head of the congregation. While we were eating, the S.S. stormed our house. They took him away while he was sitting at the table, having his Sunday meal with us. They just walked in and got him, because they hadn't found him in church that morning.

The S.S. saw any kind of gathering as a threat, whether it was religious or not. Absolutely no meetings of any kind, anywhere, were allowed, other than the Mussolini gatherings for the children, or they were accused of being American spies.

I started crying and shaking my head *no* when they arrested Papa. Another member of the church lived right next door. At first, the guards stormed his house to take him, and his daughter ran out to see Papa. She was crying out, "The guards are at our house! They're taking our father!" Mama, being the pastor's wife, ran to the house next door, to console the wife. While she was out, the guards stormed our house, and took *her* husband. She ran home and she found that her husband, too, had been taken. It was a very traumatic moment. Papa was the sole breadwinner, and that's when we kids started foraging through the fields, looking for roots and vegetation to take home and eat. We were starving.

When Papa was in prison, the guards were very harsh. Papa kept his ministerial attitude; he was kind to them and talked to them about the Lord. When he talked to the guards about the Lord, the others listened to him say that Jesus died on the cross for us. He was eking out a living because of his religion, and because he was a shoemaker. He said the imprisonment was all wrong.

The German guards and inmates made fun of him, and told him, "Look, are you going to be a shoemaker and a pastor, scraping for a living? Come with us. You're so eloquent, with a good heart. People believe in you, and you know how to talk to people. We can teach you how to be a con man, and earn a much better living separating people from their money. It's better work than preaching the gospel."

Papa would tell them, "That is not what I am, and that is not my calling in life."

When the war and fascism ended, the German commanding officers left Italy, and the younger, lower ranked soldiers were left behind; they had lost the war and they had no transportation back to Germany. So, the children who befriended them earlier recognized the young soldiers and invited them to their houses. They stayed in our house, too. We shared the little bit of food we had with them.

Strangely enough, two houses down, the Vatican sent four high-ranking American soldiers to stay there undercover. The human heart of the Italian people prevailed over the politics of fascism. Our poor families opened our hearts and homes to these soldiers to give them refuge, even though the Italian people were oppressed by the S.S.

I think people in the United States have taken their eyes from the goals of the Founding Fathers. They're becoming very materialistic, with too much emphasis given to comfort, versus the things of the heart and people's personal relationship with the Maker. When you start taking God out of the schools and the courtrooms, something has to take its place... in its place is evil.

Mussolini was an atheist, but he became baptized in the Catholic church simply to get some credibility with the Italian people. He never believed – it was a false baptism. It was a baptism of convenience.

The consequences of walking away from the fundamentals of the laws of faith, morals, and the Ten Commandments, is walking away from the Giver of all good things, the Giver of peace and love. You walk away from that. You get men eating each other up, killing each other, allowing the evil things to take over their lives when God has no part in society.

The Founding Fathers created the Constitution, the laws, and the freedom of man to express themselves under the freedom of God. That's why we say "In God We Trust." If you take that trust in God away, where do you put the trust... in man? Man is frail, and he fails without the guidance of the Higher Power. That's why the Founders believed in a nation of laws, not a nation of men. When you have a nation of men, you have a lust for power and oppression. It's arrogant of man to think they can do it better than God. When people believe that, they allow themselves to be dazzled by possessions and human things. That's when the evil comes in.

I'm afraid that socialism is taking over the world. The way to destroy one society is to allow other nations to dictate what their society can do. For instance, what does the European Union have to do with anything we decide to do in Italy? When Obama went to Denmark to sign this pact to supposedly stop or slow down global warming, that would allow other countries to dictate to the United States.

Never has a president of the United States bowed down to anyone when greeting them. And Obama bowed to the Emperor of Japan, in front of the Arab kings. That's not right. That brings America down.

What does the United States need to have? Liberty. You've got to give people liberty. You don't have to impose on them top to bottom. Get the government out of people's lives. Socialism wants to control everything. This administration, both in the White House and in Congress, is the closest I have ever seen to the socialist era, to what Mussolini did to Italy.

Fabio (Anna's Son)
*"The United States was not meant to be a
socialist country. I think America is waking up."*

I WAS BORN IN ROME in 1950, and left Italy for America in 1969, when I was barely nineteen years old. The United States had closed immigration and it was easy to go to Canada, so I went to there. I lived in Toronto until 1977; then I moved to San Diego for another three years, and came to San Francisco in 1980. I left Italy all by myself with two bags and sixty bucks in my pocket. I just hopped on a plane with a one-way ticket to Toronto – it was really an adventure. I wanted something different, to go to the land of the free. I started living in freedom – freedom! That's why I came.

My reaction was, why can't the people back home live like this? It's so free here – why does there have to be so much dog-eat-dog back home, just to beat the system? That's the way it's becoming here. Why does it have to be that way? That's why I'm a true American, by choice. It's in my system. I named my little dog Jenna Barbara, after the Bushes' daughters, but sometimes I call her Jenna Lollobrigidog.

Until 1968, Aldo Moro was the Prime Minister of Italy – it was more center-right. But there was a lot of corruption, and after his second term as Prime Minister, he was kidnapped and murdered by the Communist Red Brigade in 1978. When I left Italy, it was during the hippie years. I wasn't that involved in politics – I more involved with school and the freedom from leaving Italy.

When I left Italy, my first reaction was, isn't it wonderful how much freedom these people have in America and Canada? These people are taking so many things for granted that are their right to have, and other countries don't have. The free markets, how free people were. How easy it was to open a little store. In Italy, just to get a telephone, in 1969, took six months to a year! The telephone company was government controlled.

Hitler came into power after Germany lost the First World War, and they were in desperate economic conditions. That's how Hitler and Mussolini came to power. In 2008, America was not really down on its knees. However, I believe the media made things look so bad with President Bush that the American people *thought* we were on our knees, and thought we were broke. They said we had the worst economy in forty years, but we had an unemployment rate of around 4.5 percent. Look at what we have now, not even counting the self-employed people, or those who gave up looking for work.

Obama came in as the savior, as the one who was going to solve all the problems, and that he was going to walk on water. That's exactly what Mussolini did to Italy. That's exactly what Obama is doing – and has done – to the United States.

For years, the Progressives have been working on our youth, and now they're of voting age. But there are some kids who are conservative, rebelling against their parents. I heard another way they're becoming more conservative is that they're against abortion. They're starting to believe in no sex before marriage. They're becoming more conservative than their parents! It's wonderful. They're so competitive and creative. I don't think some guy who's over forty is going to beat that competitiveness out of them. People have a truly competitive nature, and they set the bar high. The progressives don't raise the bar any more – they want everybody to be the same.

Our Founding Fathers gave us some wonderful instruments called the Bill of Rights, the Constitution, and the Declaration of Independence – all men are created equal. But not infallible – equal. The Constitution is the instrument that helps us with our fallibility.

That's what made our country great – the low taxes, keeping the government out of our bedrooms, our living rooms, our churches, and letting us, the citizens, with our God-given feelings of wanting liberty and the pursuit of happiness, the freedom of letting that happen. If something goes wrong, we can tell ourselves that there's something wrong and we shy away from it. That's why the free market works.

I do see parallels between what's happening now and my mother's experiences during World War II. It definitely evokes a spirit of sadness in my heart, because this is not what America is all about. This is not what our Founding Fathers had in mind for us.

The good thing is that there's been a certain awakening. People are saying, "No, wait a minute. Stop!" That happened somewhat in Italy, but after being beaten so many times in the First and Second World Wars, and what Mussolini did to the country, most of them did not have the energy to fight. Their houses had been bombed, and family members were killed. They didn't have what it took to fight back. It took American soldiers to rebuild Europe, and rebuild Rome, my hometown.

The spirit of America came to help, paid for with the lives of our brave and beautiful soldiers. That spirit is now being attacked from within! And now we have to go to Europe and apologize? We rebuilt Germany. We rebuilt Japan. We rebuilt Europe. And Obama goes there to apologize!

To avoid going down the same path, I'd say don't use newspapers and TV as your only source of information, because most of the time it's a liberal media. Follow your natural instinct of wanting liberty, and don't depend on the government. As a nation, we should clean up Washington, because there's a tremendous amount of corruption in both parties.

I've heard it said that we should have four-year term limits: two in office and two in jail.

Put people in Washington who are almost volunteering their time, and do away with lifetime political careers. No fabulous pensions, no fabulous health plans, no nothing. Get businesspeople in Washington and clean up both houses... not career politicians. Jefferson wanted us to have a citizen government. Most of these people have never had to meet a payroll, or go out and shop for health insurance. They're detached. How can they run a country if they're so detached from our reality?

I saw part of the health care debate on C-SPAN, and it struck me that a lot of those people are better qualified to run the country than Obama. They've met the responsibility of working in the free market – Obama's never done anything like that. Never had to meet a payroll, or keep up with competition. He ran on a very middle of the road philosophy and platform, and when he came into office, he went totally to the left.

I believe the Tea Party movement should reform the GOP and be their conscience, not be in opposition to it. We don't need a third party – we just need a revitalized Republican party. My wish would be to have the GOP reform itself enough that it attracts the Tea Party movement. The Progressives have taken over the Democratic Party – that's not good at all. We need to get rid of the corruption and the bad politicians. Clean up both parties.

There was a high level of corruption during the Mussolini era within the higher ranks of government. The elite could do anything they wanted. There was no middle class, just the poor working folks. The corruption within the poor working folks was just to survive. The elites thought they could do no wrong. It's like Nancy Pelosi and all the money she's spending on the biggest jet any House speaker has ever had. That kind of corruption, abnormal behavior as far as decadence and opulence.

Taking somebody's land... my family on my father's side were large landowners in Rome, and Mussolini came and just took our land. The stadium where the Summer Olympics were held in 1960 – that was our land! We had apartment buildings, too. My great-grandparents had that land, and it was taken away from them under Mussolini. That's the kind of corruption that was there.

In Italy, they have socialized medicine. You have to wait in line to get any kind of examination – even to this day. It took my mother months to get an appointment for a colonoscopy. She finally got the appointment the day after Christmas in 2008 – nobody wanted that day because of the preparations. Nobody wanted to ruin their Christmas.

The day after her colonoscopy, she started feeling sick and called the doctor. He wouldn't make house calls even though she was sick in bed. After he refused to come five times, a family member went over to his office and said, "You *are* coming to the house! This woman is not well." My mother's abdomen was hard as a rock; he called the ambulance and they

had to remove a portion of her colon. The technician rup-
tured her colon during the colonoscopy; because of this and
the subsequent untreated infection, a portion of her intestine
and colon had to be removed. This is why she now has a permanent bag. Thank you, socialized medicine.

My brother said there wasn't anything we could do. She
was ruined for life. You can't sue a doctor in Italy. You sign an
affidavit, waiving all your rights to sue; otherwise, they won't
perform any procedures.

I couldn't watch the health care summit. I had to read
about it, because I just can't watch Obama. It's a visceral feeling I have – his posture and seeing his chin go up reminds me
of Mussolini's posture. America has spoken about the health
care bill, and they don't want it. The administration couldn't
care less. I believe they have an agenda to socialize this country to bring us down to the rest of the world, but that's no
good for our country. They're the elites, and they think they
know what's best for our country.

The United States was not meant to be a socialist country. I
think America is waking up. I put a lot of trust in the American spirit, in the American way. We have these good hearted
but nevertheless misguided left-wingers who want insurance
for everybody, but they're going to be outnumbered pretty
soon. I think they really believe that this is the best thing for
the country. I don't think they set out to destroy this country.
They just subscribe to ideas that are destructive.

Four

IRAQ

"We played a soccer match against Uday Hussein's team. We scored sixteen goals, but the referee counted only six, because he didn't want us to be hanged in the main plaza."

*Bassil Kamas (back row, second from left)
in Baghdad College, 1979.
(Photo: Courtesy Bassil Kamas)*

Iraq

CONSIDERED THE WORLD'S FIRST CIVILIZATION, Mesopotamia got its start around 3500 BC, in the area now known as Southeastern Iraq. After being conquered by the Persians in 539 BC, Mesopotamia was ruled by a long succession of invaders, including Alexander the Great in 332 BC, the Parthians in 126 BC, Arab Muslims in 633 AD, Mongol invaders in 1258, the Ottoman Empire around 1500, and finally as a protectorate of Great Britain in the 1800s.

In 945, a group of Shi'ite Muslims invaded Baghdad and the ruling Abbasid Empire was reduced to nothing more than a shell government. Regional authority over the country was assumed by different Muslim sects until the 16th century.

On March 11, 1917, Baghdad was occupied by British troops. Following the end of World War I hostilities, the San Remo Peace Conference of Allied Powers mandated that control over the country be given to Britain, along with control over Palestine and Transjordan in April 1920. The former Ottoman provinces of Baghdad, Basra, and Mosul became known as Iraq.

A tribal revolt took place throughout the territory in June of 1920, due to High Commissioner Sir Arnold Wilson's refusal to allow any Iraqi autonomy. He was replaced by Percy Cox, who held a softer perspective concerning Iraqi involvement in Iraq's affairs.

Iraq became an independent state on October 3, 1932, under the monarchy of King Faisal I, but was subject to the provisions of the Anglo-Iraqi Treaty that gave Britain certain rights for the following twenty-five years.

However, after various coups and assassinations in the 1930s, the treaty was ended in April of 1941 as the government began to express support for Nazi Germany. In June, the British occupied Iraq once again.

In May 1953, Faisal II became king of Iraq, and in February of 1955 he signed a treaty with Iran, Turkey, Britain, and Pakistan that purported to achieve economic and military cooperation. However, many viewed the treaty as an effort to split Arab countries apart, and Saudi Arabia, Jordan, and Syria signed a counterpact as a response.

On December 1, 1956, martial law was declared by King Faisal II and the parliament was suspended. He and the Crown Prince were killed in July 1958 in a coup led by Colonel Abd-al-Salam Muhammed Arif and General Abd-al-Karim Qassim, who then declared Iraq to be a republic. Another coup was attempted in March 1959, led by Colonel Abdel Wahab Shawaf, who alleged that the government was heavily dominated by Communists.

Ba'athist rebels failed in another coup attempt on October 7, 1959. Seventy-eight rebels were captured and tried, but one of them escaped into Syria. His name was Saddam Hussein.

On February 8, 1963, Abd-al-Salam Muhammed Arif and the Arab Socialist Ba'ath Party launched a successful coup against Iraq President Qassim; Arif installed himself as the new president. General Qassim was executed by firing squad the next day. Just ten days later, Arif purged the very same Ba'athists from his own administration who had assisted in the coup against Qassim, creating a new government supportive of Egyptian President Gamal Abdel Nasser. After Arif died in a helicopter crash in April of 1966, his older brother Abd-al-Rahman Muhammed Arif became the new Iraqi leader.

On July 17, 1968, Ba'athists once again launched a coup against the Arif government. This time they were successful, and installed General Ahmad Hasan-al-Bakr as president and Saddam Hussein as vice president. In February 1970, Iraq signed a fifteen-year treaty of "friendship and cooperation" with the Soviet Union.

Saddam Hussein replaced President Bakr on July 16, 1979, amid claims of health problems. (Bakr was placed under house arrest and died in 1982, allegedly due to poisoning.)

War between Iraq and Iran broke out on September 22, 1980, over territorial disputes. In March 1988, chemical weapons were used again the Kurdish town of Halabja, including the nerve agents sarin, VX, tabun, soman, and mustard gas. Saddam blamed Iran for the five-hour attack which killed close to five thousand Kurdish citizens, and injured another eleven thousand.

The Iran-Iraq War lasted until July 20, 1988, when Iran's Ayatollah Khomeini agreed to a cease fire.

Iraq invaded neighboring Kuwait on August 2, 1990. The U.N. Security Council issued Resolution 660 condemning the action and calling for Iraq's withdrawal, but Hussein ignored the resolution. U.S.-led coalition forces began attacks on January 17, 1991, ultimately driving Iraq's forces completely out of Kuwait. A cease fire was reached on March 3, and hostilities formally ended on

April 10, 1992. The Iraq National Assembly officially acknowledged Kuwait's sovereignty in November 1994.

After growing evidence of Iraq's continual development of internationally banned weapons of mass destruction – including the execution of two of Saddam Hussein's sons-in-law who attempted to defect with direct evidence – American and British forces invaded Iraq via Kuwait on March 20, 2003. This was the start of the second Gulf War, and the use of the tactic of suicide bombing. Iraqi vice president Taha Yassin Ramadan announced that suicide bombings would become "routine military policy."

That July, after U.S. forces were tipped off by an Iraqi citizen, Saddam's two brutal sons Uday and Qusay were found and killed after a four-hour-long gun battle with U.S. troops in Mosul. Task Force 20, a military unit created to apprehend Saddam and his top people, received support from the 101st Airborne Division and other special forces in the operation.

On December 13, 2003, Saddam Hussein was finally captured by U.S. forces in Operation Red Dawn. He was found hiding in a "spider hole" beneath a two-room mud shack on a sheep farm near his home city of Tikrit. Despite ongoing hostilities, Iraq's governing council unanimously approved a new constitution on March 8, 2004. In June, the Iraqi interim government and Prime Minister Iyad Allawi accepted sovereignty from the U.S. government, and Iraq took legal custody of Saddam Hussein. In October 2005, Saddam went on trial in Iraqi court, facing charges of crimes against humanity. That month, Iraqi voters approved a new constitution, and in December, millions of purple-fingered Iraqis cast ballots for a new government and parliament.

Saddam Hussein was found guilty of crimes against humanity in November 2006, and was executed by hanging on December 30 of that year. January 2007 saw President Bush's announcement of a troop surge to support security in Iraq.

Saddam's cousin Hasan al-Majid, also known as "Chemical Ali" was found guilty of planning the Halabja massacre, and was hanged by an Iraqi court in January 2010. Two months later, 60 percent of Iraqi voters took part in their second parliamentary election since the fall of Saddam Hussein.

Bassil Kamas

"During Saddam's regime, if you didn't stick your nose into the government's business, usually nobody bothered you."

IRAQ IN THE SIXTIES and Seventies was a pretty nice place to be in, aside from the coups and regime changes. The people were educated, and many people came from other Arab countries to study in our universities. Iraqis are highly educated, and because of the English colonization, English became the second language.

I was born in Baghdad in 1962, and we had a good childhood living in the country. My mother was a homemaker, and my father was a somewhat successful contractor, building roads and things like that. He had his own business, as well as a shop in his garage, where he fixed Caterpillars, the big construction machinery. I wouldn't say we were rich, but we had what we needed, and a little more. We had a driver, a garden-

er, and we used to go to Lebanon every summer until the civil
war became bad. Then we started going to England every
summer, because my grandmother and my aunt lived there.

Living in Iraq was actually a positive experience until Saddam
Hussein took over. During Saddam's regime, when I was in
my early teens, if you didn't stick your nose into the government's business, usually nobody bothered you.

However, it was also chaotic there – if your neighbor
didn't like you, they could just go to the government or the
MANM, the secret police, and say, "So-and-so is having meetings every night, and I think they're going to overthrow the
government." Then, the police came and took you without
any questions. Even if you thought you lived peacefully, it was
very chaotic, because they don't ask questions. They just take
you.

Every neighborhood had a Ba'ath Party house, where they
watched the neighborhood. You see them twenty-four hours a
day, sitting in the driveway, driving in and out, changing
crews. If you had a visitor from another city, they'd park their
car in front of your house for a couple of days. The watchers
would knock on your door and ask, "Who's this, and why is he
here?" But they didn't usually bother you unless you spoke
out against the regime.

That happened to my mother once. My young cousin was
taking medication for schizophrenia, and he stayed with us
for a little while. Once, he missed a couple of his daily doses.
He went into the Party house and told them, "My aunt is having meetings." The MAMN came and took her – she actually

went to the chambers and met with Saddam, face to face. She was smart enough to bring my cousin's medications and his doctors' papers, because she had a feeling that he turned her in. She's only five-two, a small lady. She stood in front of Saddam, who said, "I understand you're having meetings."

She replied, "No, Mr. President. Look at me, I'm five-foot-two – what am I going to do to overthrow a government?" He asked for the papers, and after she showed him everything, he allowed her to go home.

She was one of the lucky ones because she actually made some sense to him. Sometimes, you didn't even get to talk to Saddam –you just went straight to jail. After a few weeks, you're out... but by then, you've been tortured.

I was fortunate to go to a private high school, called Baghdad College. It was an American school, and had been owned by American missionaries. I went to the same school with Saddam's son Uday, the crazy one. It was probably one of the best schools in the country – and the safest – because Uday never went around by himself. He always had four or five bodyguards with machine guns, so everybody stayed away from that school – there was no trouble. It was a very safe school.

We had a big soccer league in the school, and all the classes played against each other. Once we played a soccer match against Uday Hussein's team. We scored sixteen goals, but the referee counted only six, because he didn't want us to be hanged in the main plaza. Uday was very angry that we beat his team. That was the only way we could get our anger out against the government, by beating his son.

We went to England every summer, and my parents always had a vision: when Saddam took over, the country would not go anywhere. I think history shows that Iraq kept declining and declining. My parents sent my two oldest brothers to England with my aunt and my grandmother, and they studied there. Now, my oldest brother lives in Ireland, and is married to an Irish girl. He's an Irish citizen now, and he's been there for almost twenty-two years. My second brother lives in Germany, works for UPS, and is a German citizen.

My youngest brother ended up in England, and I ended up in America. I came to here in 1980, but before that, I visited in 1978. When my parents said it was time for me to go to England with my brother, I said, "I don't think so. I think I'm going to America." They asked why. I was sixteen in 1978, and when I visited America, I saw one thing I never saw in all of Europe. I saw a sixteen-year-old driving a car, and it was *his* car. When they asked me what that meant, I said, "That means America is the land of opportunity." I still think that's true.

So they said okay. I ended up in Regal Park, New York, on August 28, 1980, and stayed with my uncle there for almost a year. I hated it because I'm a very friendly guy, and I didn't know any of my neighbors. For me, coming into New York was a wonderful experience. But all I heard were sirens going all day long, and I had all these visions of crimes in New York.

I called my aunt, who was living in Citrus Heights, California, at the time, and asked, "Do you know your neighbor?"

"Yes."

"Do you know your neighbor's neighbor?"

She said, "Yeah."

"Do you know your neighbor's neighbor's neighbor?"

"Yeah, of course."

"Do you have an extra room?"

She said, "Yes."

"I'm coming over."

So I packed my stuff and went to California, and I've been here ever since. I've lived in Arizona, San Diego, and San Francisco, but the majority of the time, I've lived in the Sacramento area.

When I first came to New York in 1978 from Iraq, I had a neck ache just from looking up at all these tall buildings – my goodness! My uncle had a cab. So, when he picked me up from the airport, he said, hey, let's look around. I had the pleasure of going to the 107th floor of the World Trade Center, the Empire State Building, and the Statue of Liberty. It was *amazing!* And I was always looking for cowboys. I asked my uncle where they were. He laughed and said, "Son, they don't have cowboys in New York."

But that's what I saw on TV – cowboys and Indians and stuff. But it was still wonderful. It's a whole new civilization. Even now, I still look at people and am friendly to them. I noticed that people in New York walk around with tunnel vision, and they keep to their own.

Moving here wasn't as much of an adjustment for me because I went to an American school and I've been to Europe. I spoke the language really efficiently, with a little more accent than I have today. I seemed to blend in with people pretty well. My parents always told me I should make friends with people, and if I wanted to be successful any place, I should stick with the natives and talk to them. Most of my Arab friends are always surrounded by their other Arab friends and talk to them in Arabic. I always hung out with my American friends, and wanted to understand the culture, learn the language.

I met my first American friend in Sacramento, a really nice Mormon kid. He was an avid fisherman, and he took me fishing at Folsom Lake when it still had water. He injected a worm with air, put it on the hook, and dropped it in the water. He looked at me and asked, "Do you know why I just filled the worm with air?"

I said, "Yes, to make it look like Dolly Parton to attract the fish."

He burst out laughing and asked, "How long have you been here?!"

"Just a few months."

He said, "You know, I think you'll do fine in this country." That was the first joke in English I ever told.

In Iraq, business owners were fine, as long as you didn't stick your nose in the government's business. I was too young to really know about that. When I came to America, I didn't understand the stock market, interest rates, and mortgages until I was about twenty-five. When I was sixteen in Iraq, I really didn't understand what my dad went through dealing with permits, bureaucracy, and red tape for his business. My nephews also have their own businesses, and they were doing fine. You work hard, and you try to create a solid foundation.

The story of how my father passed away is extraordinary. He bid on a contract and got it, which meant a couple other men who were close to the government didn't get it. They invited him to dinner and told him they wanted the contract. My father told them that he won the bid fair and square. And the next thing you know, they poisoned my dad, and that's how he passed away. They were close to people in the government, and they got away with murder.

My father sat with them during the business dinner, and came home and told my mom, "I just told them no." A couple of hours later, he felt really sick and was throwing up blood. My mother took him to the hospital at three o'clock in the morning, and he passed away by five..

They found poison in his body, but these people got away with murder. This was in the early Eighties, and I was here in America. I was about thirty-six, and I was eighteen the last time I saw my dad. When I left Iraq, I couldn't go back and see him, and he couldn't come and see us. We talked on the phone regularly. We were physically far apart, but emotionally, we're a very close family, always close. I couldn't even go back for the funeral.

I left Iraq under the radar – twenty days after I came to America, the Iran-Iraq War started. My mother's Iranian, and my father's Iraqi. That would have put me on the front lines because I'm not pure. I guess I escaped.

I know people are worried about the direction the United States is taking. Even when Abu Graib happened, I always thought, America has great principles. At the end of the day, there are always checks and balances. A congressman takes a bribe, eventually he will get caught. A politician lies to millions of people, he will be impeached. I always thought the principles were always great. There will always be people who will use and abuse their power for their own purposes. But, the principles that this country stands on are almost foolproof, and things will always come out in the open.

Everywhere, there's going to be good and bad; everywhere, there's going to be corruption and bribery. But I honestly believe that at the end of the day, nobody's going to come to my house and say, "You know, we're going to take you to jail because somebody said this about you." Unless they have proof of something I did, then I'm not going to be accused falsely. I've been here twenty-nine years, and never once have I been falsely accused. Even when I get pulled over by a highway patrolman, they're always nice and polite, and they always make sure that they're fair. Every time I've gotten a ticket, it's always been my fault.

I think the principles of this country are so strong that at the end of the day, things will always work for the best.

Someone said to be wary of asking the government for things, because what it gives to you, it will also take away. You're ceding a lot of your self-determination and handing it over piece by piece by piece to the "benevolent control of the government." Just in the first four months of the Obama's new administration, so many things happened so quickly.

I remember one of Obama's campaign speeches, where he said we needed to have a civilian security force as large and well-funded as the nation's military – that sounded *big* alarms with me. Firing a bank CEO, deciding what General Motors is going to do, what Fiat's going to do. I see the government doing things so quickly, things that it had never really done before, because now it *can*. I think that's unprecedented, since FDR was in office, and there are so many government fingers in what should be private business and private decisions.

I agree that the Obama administration is sticking its nose into private business, has more control, and is taking more money and taxes and everything. But I honestly think that either a Republican or Democratic government has one thing in mind, to take as much as they can. To have the money is to have power, really. The taxes hardly ever go down, and we're just paying and paying and paying. I think either party is in the same boat. They take turns in power, and we all end up doing the work.

I think once you hit people in the pocketbook, people who are educated about the subject, especially business owners, they're going to say, "Wait a minute! We can't have this!" I have a business, so I understand. Where is my money going? I think the growing frustration might have a positive outcome because more people will get involved, and be aware of how the government affects their lives.

But there's a whole slew of people that just float in this country. As long as they have twenty bucks in their pocket for the weekend, a six-pack and maybe a joint, they don't care. They might not understand – they think their tax refund is extra money from the government. They don't see it as their money that they paid in taxes during the year, and then the government said, oh okay, here's some of your money back.

There are always people who just don't know what's going on. On 9/11 I stayed in front of the TV just to watch and watch and watch, get the news, and organize in my mind what happened. Finally, after six or seven hours, I went out just to drive. This guy pulled up right next to me, and he was listening to rap music – *loud*. And it hit me, you know, this guy will not even know that 9/11 happened for probably three more days, because he's just somewhere else, on a whole different planet. They don't even know; they don't understand where their money's going, where it's coming from.

When I came first to this country, I was driving with my aunt and saw an unemployment line. I asked what it was. She told me it's for people who don't work, and who get government assistance.

I told her, "You know what? They're only eighteen, nineteen years old. I will never stand in the unemployment line, and I will never stand in the welfare line." I will never do that, and that's it. I've always had a job when some of my American friends didn't have jobs. I didn't have a work permit. I was still working, and they didn't have jobs. Of course, they wasted a lot of time and money. There's a whole group of people who just live for the weekend – that's the high point in their lives.

(People shouldn't be afraid of taking responsibility for themselves. When you have a chance to fail, and pick yourself up and do it again, it's that much sweeter, and you learn more... much more than just having it given to you.)

While at the NATO Summit in Istanbul, Turkey, on June 28, 2004, National Security Advisor Condoleezza Rice passed this note to U.S. President George W. Bush. The note read: *"Mr. President, Iraq is sovereign. Letter was passed from Bremer at 10:26 AM Iraq time. – Condi."* Upon reading it, President Bush wrote on the note, *"Let freedom reign!"*

.

Five

IRAN

*"Freedom is in our blood. You might not know what it means.
But you do know that living in a society where you're afraid to
speak your mind – it's not right."*

Family passport photo, 1987.

Iran

BETTER KNOWN AS PERSIA until 1935, Iran's recorded history stretches back past 500 B.C. For over a thousand years, the Persians successfully expanded their empire into far-flung regions such as the lower Danube and even India. Persian armies marched on Greece, conquered Athens, and battled the Romans and the Huns.

Arabic and Islamic influences in Persia began around 650 AD, after several major cities fell to Arab assaults with losses totaling over 120,000. The "golden age" of the Islamic Empire (8th to 10th centuries) owed much to the contributions of Persian science and literature, much of which was borrowed from former interactions with Greece.

The Mongol army of Genghis Khan invaded in 1221, and by 1258, his grandson Hulagu Khan succeeded in completely subduing the whole of Persia, which was then considered to be a territory of the Great Khan of China.

Persia was ruled by a succession of dynasties for the next six hundred years, enduring civil religious conflicts among various Islamic sects, assassinations and coups, and skirmishes with Russia, Armenia, and Georgia.

In 1848, Shah Naser od-Din began a "modernization" effort by greatly increasing trade with Great Britain. However, Muslims objected to this new Western influence, and the Shah was assassinated in a mosque.

In 1900, Shah Muzzaffar ed-Din awarded the British the right to develop newly discovered Persian oil reserves. After widespread civil unrest in 1906, a new constitution and a Persian parliament were introduced. Upon ed-Din's death in 1907, the parliament came to an end when Shah Muhammed Ali came into power. After his death two years later, his son Sultan Ahmed continued the attempted ouster of Westerners and their influence, with the help of twelve thousand Russian troops.

The last Persian dynasty (Pahlavi) began in 1925, when the military officer Reza Khan seized power. After a negotiated acceptance by the clergy which also rejected a Persian republic, Shah Reza began a new campaign of modernization and changed the country's name to Iran. By 1935, many vestiges of religious authority had been outlawed, including the wearing of traditional veils. In 1941, Reza was finally deposed by Russian and British interests, and replaced by his son Muhammed Reza.

After resisting a second constitutional revolution, the Shah created the secret police known as SAVAK in 1957, and the Ayatollah Khomeini was jailed in 1963. He was released in 1964, and resumed his public criticism of the Shah, even after being exiled to Najaf in Iraq.

In 1971, Iran bought four billion dollars of U.S. arms to counter Soviet influence in the region; this expenditure was soon followed by decreased oil revenue that led to a budget deficit and economic hardships. In 1978, Khomeini relocated to Paris, where he gained the attention of the international press. After Khomeini called for an Islamic Revolution in Iran, the Shah left the country on January 16, 1979, and Khomeini returned on February 1st as the Supreme Leader.

The first seizure of the U.S. Embassy in Tehran by the new Islamic Republic occurred on February 14th, followed by a second on November 4th, along with the taking of fifty-three American hostages by Iranian militants and students. The Ayatollah justified these actions as necessary to unify the country. American President Jimmy Carter was unable to secure the release of the hostages during his term in office.

Iraq invaded Iran on September 22, 1980, and after 444 days of captivity, the hostages were finally released on January 20, 1981, the day Ronald Reagan was sworn in as U.S. President. In July 1988, Iran agreed to honor a U.N. resolution that called for the cessation of hostilities with Iraq. Ayatollah Khomeini died on June 4, 1989, and was replaced by Ayatollah Khamenei.

Iran soon earned the designation as a state sponsor of terrorism, and was subjected to sanctions from the U.S., United Nations, and the European Union due to its worldwide activities and nuclear ambitions.

Although there was a brief period of reform in the government between 1997 and 2004, the controversial election of Mahmoud Ahmadinejad in 2005 established him as a "hard-liner" president. His reelection in 2009 sparked widespread nationwide allegations of fraud. Since then, Ahmadinejad has also rejected five U.N. resolutions calling for Iran's suspension of reprocessing and enrichment of nuclear materials and ballistic missile programs.

Anahita H.

"Look at the Basij, the citizen army in Iran. They are more brutal, more covert, more dangerous than any group I have ever known... because you don't know who they are."

AROUND THE TIME OF the Islamic Republic Revolution, my family lived in Ilam, a small province by the Iraqi border. Since most of the deaths, destruction, and violence took place in Tehran, my family didn't witness the Revolution that much, however, they felt it. Because both of my parents worked for the government, they were forced to resign. Their positions weren't controversial enough for the new government to fear retaliation from them.

Prejudice toward other religions and cultures was soaring. I believe non-Muslims and non-Persians were denied access to government jobs. In the first few years of the Islamic Republic, it was really bad and the laws were really strict. *Prisoner of Tehran*, by Marina Nemat, is a great eyewitness account by a teenager who was on the receiving end of prejudicial acts. She nearly lost her life as a result. The Islamic Republic was so focused on rooting out and squashing their opposition that they arrested first and asked questions later. You were accused, arrested, forced to give names, and possibly killed if you didn't cooperate. Many times, the accusations were baseless and stemmed from the testimonies of scared teenagers who just gave random names in order to protect their own lives.

I was born in Tehran on Anahita Street. I was going to be named Azadeh, which means "Freedom." I was born around the beginning of the Iran-Iraq War, so my parents didn't think it was appropriate to name me Freedom and went with Anahita at the very last minute. Anahita is a Zoroastrian goddess, and, according to some teachings, Zoroastrianism is the oldest monotheistic religion in the world.

After the Revolution, they changed most of the street names to Muslim names, because they didn't want any pagan names. The last time I was in Iran, though, the street I was born on was still the same, and there are still several other Anahita Streets left in the city.

I was born early in the morning, and the power had gone out because there were air strikes. The nurses didn't want to deliver me yet because the power was out, and it was hard for them to proceed, so they tried to tie up my mother's legs. They hoped that would delay the birth. She went nuts on them and wouldn't let them, and she flailed her legs so they couldn't tie them. She was in labor for twenty minutes at the most. Had they been successful in tying up her legs, I probably would have suffocated during birth.

I joke that I'm a MINO – Muslim In Name Only. Many of us in the Persian Muslim community outside the Middle East aren't considered good "practicing" Muslims because we don't cover up by wearing the hijab, we partake in libations, and some of us don't take the time to pray five times a day.

One of the things that Islam frowns upon that Persians do is being superstitious. Some of us are into astrology or fortune telling. If you go to Iran – nothing's publicized, because it's against the law – you can have someone read your coffee or tea leaves or your palm, but it's kept secret.

Unlike my siblings, I never experienced a normal society. The Revolution had taken place in 1979, so I had the war *and* the Islamic Republic hanging over my head. In Islam, technically a girl becomes a woman at the age of nine, because that's when a woman's body starts to develop. By then, girls should be covered up, but they still recommend it for younger girls. My mom went to a government building with me when I was three years old, and the guard told her, "You should be ashamed of yourself! You're raising her to be a trollop!" Three – what kind of sin could a three-year-old commit?

Originally, the belief for covering up is to protect you from the sin of others. In Islam, they believe that if it wasn't in the Book – the Qoran – look at how the Prophet Mohammed led his life. He visited the Byzantine king, and asked him why the queen was covered up. The king replied, "My wife is too beautiful for any man to take pleasure from." If another man takes pleasure from her beauty, his sin is also her sin, because she's causing him to have pleasure, even if it's indirectly. Even men aren't supposed to wear short shorts or sleeveless shirts.

I have four other siblings: six, nine, twelve, and fifteen years older than me: two boys, two girls. My mom was a teacher as well, so my siblings always had homework time. When they did homework, I wrote in my little notebook, pretending I was writing, too. Eventually my mom started tutoring me, and I learned how to read, write, and do math when I was four.

When I was five, I learned how to ride a bike. In Iran, most people had fresh milk and fresh bread for breakfast, so you'd have to wait in line each morning. The place with the milk opened up at five, and it was on a first-come, first serve basis. Because I woke up early, I rode my bicycle over to get milk for the family – so *I* was the milkman.

Our neighborhood was called Sattar Khan; we had moved away from Anahita Street when I was about three. Our block was enclosed, and there were a couple of ways out of the neighborhood. Inside our neighborhood, there were two bakeries, three delis, and a bunch of little shops. So, I just rode my bike through the neighborhood to get milk and bread, then went home. The best part was the smell of fresh bread in the morning and in the afternoons.

I was sixteen in the summer of 1986 when one of my two uncles living in the United States came to visit us for the first time in a long time. They'd been living in the U.S. since the Sixties. He had never experienced the war, but we did have an air raid when he visited. When the Iraqi planes approached, the sirens went off. We were supposed to turn off all the lights and go in the basement – when the lights are off, they can't tell if it's a city or not, and then you're not an obvious target. So, the bombers look at the geography, take guesses and go, and they didn't care if civilians were killed.

Not long after that, they got the technology for the planes to come all the way to Tehran, a little over 440 miles. The first few years, the war took place along the border provinces.

You'll see severe birth defects there because Saddam contaminated their water and soil.

Everything you've heard that Saddam didn't have chemical warfare was B.S. Iran is an example that he did have chemicals. He just hid them well. God knows where they are. It's the desert; it's like finding a needle in a haystack. One of Iran's nuclear power plants was buried, and we found it with satellite imagery technology. But it's hard to find nonreactive weapons. I don't care what anybody says. Saddam had chemicals, and they were used on Iranians.

It doesn't take much to contaminate water. My neighborhood was one of the target neighborhoods because we lived close to one of the power plants in Tehran. The portion of the city that was powered also had the airport and the military residences. There's also a neighborhood with homes and high-rises on the outskirts of Tehran. The rent and home values are discounted for active military or veterans, and they lived pretty close to our neighborhood and the power plant.

Iraqi bombers flew toward our neighborhood often – they really wanted the power plant. You could hear the bombs as they struck nearby neighborhoods, and when my uncle visited, he couldn't believe that we lived under these conditions. He said, "Are you crazy? Why are you doing living here? Get over to the U.S.!" My dad had first moved to the U.S. in 1969. The original plan was for him to find a job, and then we would all move back. He had a green card, so it wasn't that difficult for us to get ours as well. It was 1969 in Los Angeles – do I need to explain why he didn't stay?

If you compare Tehran with Los Angeles in 1969, there's no way anyone in their right mind would let their children grow up in L.A. My brother was almost three years old, and my sister was a baby. With all the "free love" and drugs prevalent in the city, my dad's protective nature kicked in when he imagined his daughter living in that environment. So, he moved back to Iran. I probably wouldn't have been born had we moved here in 1969. My parents probably would have settled with two kids since we didn't have the extended family support system in the U.S. that we have in Iran.

My other uncle living in the U.S. had the financial means, so he sponsored us. Only my mom and four of the kids moved over. We were supposed to go for our green card interviews in the winter of 1986. We went to Turkey, because there's no longer a U.S. Embassy in Iran. Our interview was scheduled for the end of the week. That Tuesday, our neighborhood was bombed. I was only five, but I remember that day vividly, because my siblings were taking a nap underneath this thing called a korsee, which is a way to conserve power and heat.

Sometimes during the wintertime, we'd keep the heat very low. The korsee is like a giant table with a heat lamp underneath it. Then we put a big, heavy blanket over the korsee, which keeps the heat in. There's padding all around it so that when the blanket is over it, you can rest on the padding, and your body fits underneath to stay warm. My siblings were taking a nap underneath it, and the power had gone out earlier that day while my mom was cooking. I went into the kitchen because she was making my favorite dish, Gormeh Sabzih (herb stew). I begged her to make it, and she told me to go take a nap. I told her I wasn't tired, so I helped her. She had arranged all of our boots and our winter coats by the door; she also had our passports, I.D. cards, everything we needed was by the door. She just had a feeling. The power had gone out, and she was being cautious. So, I went to take a nap.

Everyone woke up before me, and were already eating dinner. I heard my mom call, "Get up!" It was already dark and the power had come back on. I was so tired. My brother dragged me out and I sat down for dinner. He turned on the TV and by my second bite, the sirens went off.

My mom said, "Here we go again!" That past month Iraqi planes kept flying by our neighborhood and missing. That day, Saddam had threatened to hit our neighborhood. We turned off the TV and the lights, and we all went down to the basement. Because the power was out, most of our neighbors had left for the afternoon and evening. Our neighbor who lived in the basement had forgotten to turn his lights off when he left, so we thought he was still home. We were all huddled together and covered up in the basement, and we called out his name because we were worried. We heard the planes coming, and then we heard a bomb – it was a lot closer than all the other bombs had ever been. Then we heard – and felt – bomb number two.

Everything shattered when bomb number three hit, and we heard an extra *boom!* There were a total of five bombs that night. The first one was nine houses to our left. The second bomb fell two houses to our right. The third one hit the power plant. All the houses in the neighborhood were attached, between two to four stories each, including basements. It wasn't that far away, because we had a small block. Two houses were destroyed by one bomb, and they were all home. One family was hosting the funeral service of a family member who had been killed earlier in the month, and the other house was hosting a wedding. That one bomb killed hundreds of people, and started a fire that spread to the adjacent homes.

If I hadn't gotten up from my nap, I would have been dead. All the glass had shattered, and shot inside like projectiles. The TV blew across the room, and all the glass shot into the walls. We were very lucky to be in the basement, and that none of the glass went through our heavy coats. I remember the fires in our little neighborhood. I remember how all the windows in our neighborhood were shattered... how dark and eerie it was when we lost power. I remember the screaming, the search and rescue dogs, the dead and injured being retrieved from under the rubble, and the looters. When the bombs fell, they shut off all the entrances to our neighborhood. How did we get looters that fast?

We went up to our apartment because I was still hungry, and my mom found an apple for me. When we went back downstairs, I saw two men climbing over my neighbor's fence. When my mom questioned them, one man told her they were looking for their sister. I asked who she was , they gave a fake name, and we said she didn't live there. My mom and I screamed, "Thieves! Thieves!" They jumped off the fence and ran away.

After the bombs stopped, my brother helped our neighbors – a lot of people died. A few days later, we flew to Turkey – I was very happy to get out of there.

We arrived at my uncle's house in California to live in June 1987. We had green cards, so it wasn't an issue. My most vivid memory when we came to the United States was going to Disneyland... and the fireworks. They sounded just like bombings. We had a nice day at the park, and we stayed to watch the fireworks show. When they started, my mom put her arms around us, and pushed us all down to the ground so the bombs wouldn't hit us. She cried out, "Saddam has come for us here!" I'll never forget how scared she looked. I don't know about my siblings, but I was terrified. The pattern and the sounds were just like bombing. I was on the ground, crying. My mom was scared for us, and my uncle tried to tell us, "It's okay, it's just fireworks." It took a while to calm me down.

We lived pretty close to the park, and it took us a while to get used to the fireworks. The first few years we went to Disneyland, I left before the fireworks began. I love them now, especially now that I understand the meaning behind a fireworks show on the Fourth of July. Think of the "Star Spangled Banner": when the fireworks go off, they make the very same sounds as "bombs bursting in air."

My mom had tutored me at home, and by the time I was six, I knew fifth-grade math, but all I knew in English were "hi" and "hello." They put me in second grade and ESL for my English.

I was out of ESL by third grade and taking advanced classes three months into the new school year.

I hated my first year of school. I was miserable. Our second-grade teacher gave the lessons in English, then explained it in Vietnamese. I didn't understand English that well, and didn't understand Vietnamese at all. I was placed in an Asian class since Iran is in the Asian continent. The school district has since ended this discriminatory class structure. The teacher's assistant was American, and she helped me out with my English.

I was picked on a lot in second grade by some fifth-grade boys. My older brother was in junior high and had to walk me home. It was hard to complain because I didn't speak English that well, so I got beaten up a lot. It was a very painful year. I ran home, but they started taking their bikes to school to chase me down. Third grade was a lot better, because I spoke English better and made some friends.

The one thing I did like about Iran was the sense of family – that's one thing that's really lacking in the United States. In Iran, we kept in touch with our cousins, our second cousins, everyone. People don't do that as much in the U.S. That's declined a bit recently in Iran because of the economy. It's just not that affordable to travel to see friends and family.

There are so many personal liberties we didn't have in Iran. In Islam, it's recommended that you be covered up. Turkey is pretty much a Muslim country, and they *choose* to be covered up – it's not the law of the land. In Iran, it *is* the law of the land. I don't mind it so much in the winter. But in the summertime, it's too hot to be covered up that much. You're covered from your head to wrists and to the ankles. So, you can't just wear flip-flops and shorts underneath. You have to wear long pants or dark tights. The area around the Persian Gulf is near the equator and it gets very humid; it's really uncomfortable.

If someone walked around uncovered, that wouldn't last long – they'd be in jail. They wouldn't even make it off the plane. They would get lashings. It's against the law, as is adultery and premarital sex. If they suspected that you were dating, you would get eighty lashes. Suspicion can arise from something as simple as walking together, or sitting by each other at the movies. If you're uncovered, someone will stop you and help you. In addition to the regular police, you have the "citizen police," like Obama's proposing. In Iran, they're called the Basij. They're everywhere, all the time.

The Basij are citizens who are incentivized. The government promises to get them placement in college and a job. In return, you report friends, family, neighbors, or anyone else who is breaking the law. They formally train police, military, and national spies, but the citizen police are everyday people who report back to the government if others are doing things like talking against the regime or about toppling it. They report anything that's against the law – dating, premarital sex, adultery, homosexuality, listening to Western music, watching Western TV, and drug and alcohol use.

In Iran, people shouldn't talk about adultery, drugs, drinking, or even dating. You never know who's listening. There are underground parties that have drugs, alcohol, and fornication. The citizen police find out the details the uniformed police can't find out, but the Basij can be invited. For all you know, it could be someone you've grown up with. They'll go in, take photos, and report back to the government. The government has so much control of the people because you never know who around you is a spy.

I traveled there in the late Nineties; a relative was friends with a member of the Basiji forces, a guy who had a crush on me. He told me everything I needed to know to protect myself. He wanted me to be safe, because he knew how vocal I was about the government. He was supposed to report me, but he wouldn't. The government knew I was there; I was being watched. He said I shouldn't say anything bad about the regime in public. Sometimes when I ran errands late in the evening, he walked with me to make sure I was safe. He walked ten to twenty paces behind me or across the road, so it didn't look like we were together.

Mohammed Khatami was elected president on May 23, 1997 – the government couldn't stop it. The voter turnout was 80 percent and he received over 70 percent of the vote. He was a very popular president and left office in August 2005. Those of us who watch the regime's patterns think the government was genius by letting him get elected. Before that, the activity to topple the government had gone underground. If they got hold of you, you'd go to jail or you were killed. People pushed the limits in the early Eighties, and a lot of them were killed.

That's when the government came up with the Basij, and formed the Ministry of Intelligence, modeled after the KGB.

When Khatami was elected, people thought they were free. Khatami still met the mullahs' criteria to be president, so this was a way to get people to open up. A few years ago, Iran had the most blogs per capita of any country in the world. They're well-known for using public resources to get information out; now they use Twitter quite a bit. With the election of Khatami, people started speaking up against practices they thought were archaic. In 1997 and 1998, a lot of newspapers were founded; there were morning, afternoon, and evening editions. A lot of the papers started writing about freedom and individual rights. That way, the government found out who the protestors were – that's when people started to go missing, and were jailed or killed.

1998 was one of the bloodiest years in recent Iran history – many, many people were killed. There were so many reporters who disappeared or were found dead. A lot of people went missing and were never heard from again. By making the people believe that there was a change by electing the moderate Khatami, the government was able to find out who the opposition was and get rid of them. That was extremely significant: that eliminated the next generation of counterrevolutionaries. The problem with the current protestors in Iran is that they're not organized enough to make the changes they need. They're in their mid-twenties and thirties now, and the people who could have led a revolt now were all killed in the late Nineties. The government shrewdly let Khatami in and the people thought they were safe to speak up.

Khatami spoke at a U.N. meeting in September 1998, and extended an olive branch to President Clinton and the U.S. He had done an interview with CNN's Christiane Amanpour in January 1998, and called for a "dialogue among civilizations," including Iran and the United States. Ten days later, the Monica Lewinsky scandal broke on the Drudge Report, and Clinton was busy trying to cover up his mess. When the Islamic Republic saw that the U.S. didn't acknowledge Khatami's overture, they made Khatami rescind it.

Our government had an opportunity in 1998 to have a dialogue with Iran; Iran had to have been developing their nuclear technology in the Nineties. I believe that if Clinton wasn't so busy having affairs, and actually took the opportunity to talk with Khatami, Iran might not be such a threat right now. The first two years of Khatami's presidency was the only time that the right people were in power and the resources were there to turn Iran into an ally.

Clinton had so many great opportunities: to take out Bin Laden, to work with Iran. In the late Nineties, Iran and the United States had the same enemy: the Taliban. Khatami wanted to work with the United States to eliminate the Taliban. Clinton didn't take that opportunity and didn't recognize the Taliban as a real threat.

The Taliban are Sunni Muslims, and Iranians are Shia Muslims. Afghanistan is a Shia nation, just like Iraq; the Shias don't like having Sunnis run their country. The Taliban funded their war by selling and smuggling drugs into Iran, which is how they funded their war. Funny how drugs are a sin in Islam, but in the eyes of these terrorists, it's okay to sell them. It was in the best interest of the Iranian regime to eradicate the Taliban, but they couldn't do it alone. During that time, Iran had the most Afghani refugees in the world. They used up public resources, were unemployed, were peddling, and some were stealing. I think Iran had the right president at the time to work with the U.S., but the U.S. didn't have the right president to work with Iran.

By the time George W. Bush was elected president, the mullahs had already weakened Khatami. After that, the mullahs pretty much shut him out because they had already rooted out their opposition. I believe that Clinton was too busy with Monica to pay attention.

I think President Carter was worse than Clinton; my parents called him the devil, because his actions opened the portal for Ayatollah Khomeini to come into power. Carter brought Khomeini out of exile because, as I understood it, he wanted a lower price for Iranian oil. Iran has some of the best crude in the world because it sits on the Persian Plateau, which is very rich in minerals. Carter tried to strike a deal with Iran to get really cheap oil, and the Shah said no. Carter wanted to get him out of power, and put one of his people in. Carter didn't do his homework; he only saw that Ayatollah Khomeini was the most vocal critic of the Shah's regime, with many supporters within Iran.

The United States had CIA intelligence in Iran and knew the opposition leaders against the Shah. Allegedly, they provided weapons to the opposition revolutionaries, and funded and trained them. The people who led the Revolution weren't wealthy people who could get their hands on weaponry. It was given to them.

The Shah left Iran for the U.S. for medical treatment on January 16, 1979 (26th of Dey). The Shah's regime fell on the 22nd of Bahman, or February 11. When the Shah left, Khomeini returned and took control. The people who supported the Revolution supported Khomeini and his ideologies. They thought Iran was too Westernized, too free. Iranians were turning their backs on the religion. I doubt the people of Iran realized what they were getting themselves into.

My family was not in Tehran when the Revolution took place. They can't tell me how bad it really was, but they told me that Jimmy Carter thought that by helping Ayatollah Khomeini get into power, that he would help him in return. And what did he do? He took over the U.S. Embassy, and the 444-day hostage crisis began. Carter did more disservice to Middle Eastern affairs than any other president. The hostage crisis stemmed from the Ayatollah showing the U.S. that Iran would not be bullied by other nations: We [Iran] don't want you [U.S.] here. The Basij now train their secret army at the former U.S. Embassy; that's their big insult to the United States.

Akbar Ganji is a very vocal pro-democracy reporter, and wrote about the Chain Murders of dissident writers and intellectuals in 1998. In 2000, he traveled to Berlin to attend a conference and spoke against the Islamic Republic. When he came back, he was sentenced to prison for ten years, and beaten very badly. He was released early on appeal in 2001, and spoke up against the government a few months later. They threw him in jail again, beat him, and after a couple of hunger strikes, he was released in 2006 in poor health. He's since left Iran. The government let him survive because he had such a huge following, but it was a warning, too.

I worked for a newspaper in Iran around that time, and before I started, our editor-in-chief was thrown in jail. We didn't know why, and they released him a few years later. For the longest time, no one knew where he was. They just saw a van pull up and pull him in, and then he was gone. No one ever knew what the allegations were. Things like that happen a lot in Iran. It looks like a kidnapping, but it's the government that's taken the person away.

My sister and her family decided to visit Iran for the first time in years in June 2009. They happened to land just a few hours after the election results, before the protests began. She said the people who were fighting the protestors were Arabs – they weren't Persian. The government brought in people from the outside, most likely Hezbollah, because Hezbollah fighters are Shia, but not Persian Shias, probably from Lebanon. She said that property was set on fire, damaged, and destroyed by the government's people, not the protestors, but they blamed everything on the protestors. They damaged vehicles and launched tear gas in neighborhoods so people wouldn't come out of their homes.

My sister said the protestors were generally peaceful and unarmed. The people who were fighting them were armed. The revolutionaries in 1979 had weapons; they didn't have any in 2009. If they were armed, you might have seen a revolution. Mir Hossein Mousavi, who challenged incumbent Mah-moud Ahmadinejad, was one of the founders of Hezbollah. That tells you a lot right there. He was a prime minister of Iran during the 1980s. Under his watch, so many counterrevo-lutionaries were killed. He's just as brutal as the rest of them.

There are two factions of religious leaders in the country. Had he been elected president, I think they planned to replace the Supreme Leader. The Supreme Leader is now Ayatollah Kha-menei, who came into power after Khomeini died – Khomeini was the first Supreme Leader. The Assembly of Experts meets for several days, twice annually, and is composed of eighty-six "virtuous and learned" clerics elected for eight-year terms. The Assembly elects the Supreme Leader and has the consti-tutional authority to remove the Supreme Leader from power at any time. It hasn't happened, but it can if you have all your alliances lined up.

The president is the political leader, and the Supreme Leader is the religious leader who interprets the Qoran. In a country where religion is the law of the land, it makes sense that the religious leader is the most powerful of all.

Whoever runs Iran controls the oil money and has a lot of power. Iran has a lot of valuable natural resources. The aver-age person in Iran either lives modestly or is poor. A lot of the rationing that took place during the Iran-Iraq War might have been relaxed a little, but there is still rationing.

The people of Iran saw Mousavi as a change agent. Keep in mind that the arrests, tortures, and killings that took place under his leadership occurred when most of the current generation of Iranians were either little children or had not yet been born. The majority of the population of Iran is under the age of thirty, and he was the last prime minister of Iran, from 1981-89, before the constitutional change eliminated that post. The history of Iran taught in schools will always be what the government wants you to know. They're not going to tell you what a brutal guy Mousavi was.

The only reason I was okay with him instead of Ahmadinejad was because he would have been their last hope for change. If he was elected, when the people of Iran realized he was the same as the others, then they would be ready for a real revolution. That's when they'll know that everything that's been promised to them were lies. Then they'll find a leader, someone either from within themselves, or someone who's left the country who understands what democracy is.

They *do* want democracy. They *do* want freedom. They don't want to turn their backs on their religion, but they know what's happening to them isn't right. They don't know exactly what *is* right, but they do know that what's going on now isn't right.

I don't think anybody in Iran would be able to effect any change without being armed. No. Sorry, but you can't fight off weapons with flower power. However, I do believe if the people are pushed to the edge, they will find the means to get weapons. It may take time and covert cooperation with allies outside of the country, but where there's a will, there's a way.

Regarding the events in the United States since Obama took office, I would say the most dangerous thing by far he's ever done is call for a citizen army. It has gone almost completely unnoticed. Look at the Basij, the citizen army in Iran. They are more brutal, more covert, more dangerous than any group I have ever known... because you don't know who they are. They're a lot bigger than the CIA or FBI will ever be, because they're everyday people. They could be your neighbors, your friends, your relatives. You don't know who they are. In Iran, it's already difficult to survive, people think: If I rat out my mom, I can put a roof over my family's head; I'll put my wife and my kids over my mom. She's old.

That's the most dangerous part about what Obama is pro-posing, of anything he's ever talked about. His words about how he wants to help everybody – Obama wants you to go to school and have the taxpayers pay for it. It's his way to control your life. It's like the federal student loans, where you owe the government money for the next ten, twenty years of your life; you owe whoever's in charge of that government. Obama says that your federal student loans will be forgiven if you work for the government. You don't owe the government – you owe *him*. When you owe an individual, it's a lot more dangerous than when you owe a collective. His giving is conditional. I'll give to you if you give me what I want.

In the Islamic Republic, they own you, they control you. With what Obama's trying to do, he wants to own you, too. Our Founding Fathers framed our country so the citizens weren't indebted to any one individual running the country. Obama and his people are trying to change that. That's the most dangerous thing I've ever heard in my life. When I hear Obama give speeches about his policies, I yell at the TV. Not just because they're violating our rights, but because that's what the Islamic Republic does. When he gives his opinions and policies, I think, that's what the Islamic Republic does.

We study history so that we don't repeat the same mistakes. But, oh my God. We do it over and over again. Look at what Jimmy Carter did. It seems like people study history, but can't put the pieces together. Yes, it's a different leader, a different country, a different time, but the patterns are all the same. Why do people choose to put their heads in the sand and ignore what's staring right at them?

It would be a good exercise to make a chart of Obama's plans, his speeches, and the comparison to the Islamic Republic. I see it from him. I wonder if he studied what they did... the way he wants to control people, the promises that he makes. It's sad, it's frustrating, and it's disappointing. It's like watching the train speeding down the track towards another train, and no one's listening to me yelling "Stop!"

I know what my family has told me about the Islamic Republic and what I experienced. I don't consider myself a true expert, and an expert would probably see a lot more than I do in Obama's actions. However, I can put the pieces together, stand back, and watch the big picture.

The Islamic Republic of Iran is, in my view, the ultimate dictatorial country that hides under a guise of democracy. It has democratic elections; you can vote, but really, you don't.

Only their people are qualified for a ballot. You have to meet certain criteria and be approved by the mullahs to qualify for the ballot. A lot of women qualify for the ballot, which is cool. I think Iran has more women in government than other countries do, at least they did a few years ago. It was that way when Khatami was president. What's the point of having women in power if the Supreme Leader can overturn their actions if they doesn't meet his religious criteria? The government's going to do what the government wants. If laws don't meet the religious requirements, they'll overturn them.

I think Obama believes that we are wrong. Don't listen to the words: look at his actions. Obama's action of bowing to world leaders is an example of how he fundamentally believes that *we* are in the wrong, *we* are not the world leader, we *should not* be the world leader. He truly believes that. Are his policies put there by his radical friends? Possibly.

It's obvious to me by his actions that he truly believes what he's saying. He wholeheartedly believes he is doing the best thing for the country. He sticks his chin up in the air and talks down to us mere mortals. His actions show me that he believes he is better than us. He looks down on the rest of us.

Look at Obama during the 2010 State of the Union address. He looked down on the Supreme Court. He *talked down to the Supreme Court*. He doesn't see them as a co-equal branch; he thinks he's their boss. He doesn't respect the checks and balances of our country, or the fact that we have *three* co-equal branches of government. Remember, the Supreme Leader of Iran is way above everybody else, and my biggest fear is that Obama truly believes that he's above everybody else, too.

With all the protests, beatings, and bloodshed during the Iran protests, he said nothing. He could have said, I believe the voice of the Iranian people should be heard. We should have encouraged them. We support democracies all around the world, with fair and open elections. It took him until late Monday after the Saturday election results to express any concern about Iran. The U.K., France, and some Latin American countries said something first.

What can the average American do to preserve their freedom? Keep thinking for yourself. Question the government. There are a lot of people I don't agree with. I don't agree with conspiracy theorists, and may totally disagree with lots of other people, but they have a right to their opinions. The moment we give up that right and let someone form opinions for us, we've lost our identity. We're no longer Americans. We have a right to disagree, and that's a right I never want to lose. What a boring world it would be if I agreed with everybody around me... or if I was forced to agree with them. Don't take things at face value. In Iran, the history you learn in school is the history they want you to learn.

Push for your dreams. The way the economy is, it might seem frustrating, but keep working at it. Don't let some government servant dictate to you how you should live. If your dream after high school is to start your own business and not necessarily go to college, then do it. If you fail, oh well. At least you tried. You don't want to be fifty years old and still working for the government, wishing you took that risk and started your own business. You learn more from your failures than from your successes.

I was unemployed for most of 2009, and I learned so much about myself during that time. The way this presidency is going, they want you to dream what *they* want to dream. The beauty of America is that you get to have your own dreams. The beauty of this country is competition. We have the spirit of competition. Competition is the fuel for ingenuity.

I'm not a fast runner, I'm not a scientist, but I do love my politics, and I *love* competition. That's why campaigns are so awesome. If we didn't have competition, we wouldn't be who we are. So many people in this world don't think it's possible for them to dream. That will kill your soul. Competition is the fuel that moves this country.

The last thing is to get involved. That's the best thing. In Iran, the level of involvement you have is limited. In the U.S., we don't have a ceiling. Get involved. Right now, there are so many heated Republican primaries because some people have realized through the Tea Party Movement and so on, that they can't sit around and wait for the right leader to come along. You need to get up and do something.

Get involved, whether it's volunteering for a candidate in a race, running for office yourself, getting signatures for a ballot petition that you believe in, gathering people to make calls to Capitol Hill or your state capital about legislation, or using your expertise to help fight against bad legislation.

So, if you know something about education, and you see an awful piece of legislation being passed that affects education, get into those committee hearings and tell them what they're doing is wrong. If I had the money, I'd run for office. Don't sit back and wait for somebody else to get involved and be your voice. You need to be your own voice.

Even for people who only knew living under a repressive government, I think there is always a human instinct to be free, even if they've never known freedom. Of course there is. It's like raising an animal in a cage. The minute you open the door, the animal will fly out. If you go to Iraq, they didn't know what it meant to be free. Many Iraqis were under Saddam's oppression for a very long time.

There are around 71 million people in Iran. About 70 percent of the population is under the age of thirty; half are under twenty-five. All my generation has ever known is the Islamic Republic. The beauty of technology, satellite, and cable is that outside information can get into Iran, and people can see what freedom means. In 1998, when Iranians stood up against the government, some of them did experience freedom. They knew it was better than the conditions they were living under.

The ultimate question is, how do you define freedom? I gauge freedom by looking at the media. If the media is truly doing investigative reporting, they're not afraid to speak up against the president or the leaders when they're doing something wrong. Look at every single country that's not free. Sure, they have reporters, but they never report critically about the government. We'll always have flawed leaders, everywhere, whether they're flawed by their personal character or their ideology. Infallible humans don't exist.

We're not perfect. Sometimes our curiosity leads us down the wrong road, and sometimes down the right road. If you're free, and that upsets someone, you're not really doing any psychological or emotional damage to them.

The Qoran was written between 610-650 A.D., and what was true then isn't necessarily true now. In Iran, the law of the land is the Qoran. Sometimes you can't be too literal. Man changes and evolves, and religion should evolve with him. The Qoran doesn't talk about driving, flying, or nuclear exploration, yet Iran does those things. It's unrealistic to think that religion can be the law of the land. Religion should be the guide to morality and decency. That's the beauty of our Constitution – it gives us the opportunity to evolve with time. It was such a great outline, and didn't fill in all the blanks for us the way religion does.

Freedom is in our blood. You might not know what it means; you might not know what it takes; you might not know the process or the definitions. But you do know that what's happening now in Iran – living in a society where you're afraid to speak your mind – it's not right. You're afraid you might get killed; you might go to jail; you might get lashes. You don't know what the right thing is, but you know that what's happening isn't right. That's the human instinct of freedom.

That's the problem we're having right now with our own government in the United States – it's trying to overreach its powers. Everyone has their own definition of freedom. It's obvious that Obama's supporters think the government should do everything for you, and you would still be free. But the reality is, you're not.

Anahita (right), her brother and uncle at
Beheshte Zahra cemetery in Tehran (approx. 1985)
(Photos: Courtesy Anahita H.)

Six

VIETNAM

"Why did people leave Vietnam? Because we lived in oppression over there. Up until this day, they are oppressed."

Father Nguyen Van Ly on trial, April 2007.

Vietnam

FOLLOWING A 1,400-YEAR seesaw struggle against Chinese influence and rule that began in 111 A.D., the people of Vietnam developed their own identity that went beyond a pale version of their former Chinese-styled society. Under several dynasties, Vietnam gradually expanded while fighting off Chinese armies intent on bringing Vietnam back into the fold.

In the early 1800s, the French missionary Pierre Behaine raised a mercenary force to help the new Vietnamese emperor Nguyen Anh seize the throne with the hopes of trading and missionary privileges for France. However, the new Nguyen dynasty was suspicious of French influence, and the Roman Catholic missionaries and their Vietnamese converts were persecuted and even executed in some cases.

Following outrage from French religious groups, commercial, and military interests, Emperor Napoleon III sanctioned the launching of an 1858 naval expedition to punish the Vietnamese and force them to accept status as a French protectorate. The first naval attack at Da Nang Harbor was unsuccessful, but after a second attack further south, the court at Hue agreed to cede several provinces in the Mekong Delta to France in 1862.

Two decades later, the French launched an attack on the North, and the Vietnamese finally accepted their status as a French protectorate over the remaining territory. French colonization brought many societal improvements in transportation and communications, and contributed to the growth of commerce and manufacturing, but brought less improvement in livelihood to the individual Vietnamese. In the early 1920s, nationalist parties demanded independence. In 1930, Ho Chi Minh formed an Indochinese Communist Party, but did not achieve much revolutionary success until World War II started in 1939.

In 1940, Japan demanded and received the right to place Vietnam under military occupation, with the existing Vichy French administration restricted to figurehead authority. Seizing the opportunity, the Communists organized the Vietminh Front and prepared to create an uprising at the close of the war. When the Japanese surrendered to the Allies in August 1945, Vietminh forces arose throughout Vietnam and declared the establishment of an independent republic in Hanoi.

The restored French government did not concede independence to the Vietminh and pushed them out of the south. For more than a year the French and the Vietminh sought a negotiated solution, but the talks were unsuccessful. War between the two started in December 1946 and lasted for almost eight years.

The Vietminh waged a guerrilla-type war from the hills, while the French created a new Vietnamese government under Emperor Bao Dai, the last ruler of the Nguyen dynasty. The Vietminh forces generally lacked the strength to defeat the French, but in 1953, the Vietminh overran the fortified French base at Dien Bien Phu. A war-weary French populace pressured their government to end hostilities, and in June 1954 the Vietminh and the French agreed to negotiations in Geneva.

At the conference, the two sides accepted an interim compromise to end the war, calling for dividing the country at the 17th

parallel. The Vietminh held the North, and the French (and their Vietnamese supporters) the South. The peace lasted until 1959, when the populace held South Vietnam's President Ngo Dinh Diem responsible for the country's economic and social ills. Sensing a weak adversary, the Communists in the north resumed their war on the south.

President Diem was killed in a coup in late 1963, and the security of South Vietnam deteriorated. The situation put victory over the South within reach of the Communists. But in early 1965, U.S. President Lyndon Johnson sanctioned precision bombing of North Vietnam military targets and sent combat troops into South Vietnam to shore up the threatened regime in Saigon.

Like the French before them, the American public soon grew tired of the Vietnam War and its horrific images of carnage that they witnessed on the evening news, a first for wartime news coverage. Protesting the war became the new cause célèbre on college campuses and in Hollywood, with help from leftist activists in the United States. Ho Chi Minh observed that the North never could have defeated the American troops without the help of student unrest fomented on college campuses to influence U.S. wartime policies.

With the Vietnam War a hot topic worldwide, the U.S. administration desperately wanted to avoid the appearance of being a larger, well-equipped bully beating up on a smaller adversary. The White House attempted to micromanage the war, instead of allowing the generals in the battlefield to make the strategic decisions. Soon, there was no clear mandate for domination over the enemy, and the resulting decline in troop morale as the casualties mounted made a decisive U.S. victory elusive.

However, the U.S. intervention did cause severe problems for the Communist forces and forced them to send North Vietnamese army regulars into battle. The bloody Tet offensive in 1968 coerced the new Saigon regime of President Nguyen Van Thieu and the Johnson administration to consider a negotiated settlement with the leaders of the North.

However, Ho Chi Minh died in 1969, and was soon replaced by Le Duan. The newly elected U.S. president Richard Nixon continued Johnson's overall policy while gradually drawing down U.S. troops. After the signing of a peace accord in Paris in January 1973, there was a temporary cessation of hostilities. The agreement called for the total removal of all U.S. troops, while Hanoi agreed to recognize the Thieu regime as the nation prepared for new elections. The Paris accord soon fell apart, however, and in early 1975 the North launched a new military offensive against the South. In less than two months, the Thieu government collapsed, bringing the war to an end with the fall of Saigon.

Cindy Nguyen

"Human life is cheap. Corruption is everywhere."

I WAS VERY YOUNG when the Communists took over my country in 1975, when the Vietnam War ended. The Communists called it "the blood-soaked war against the Imperialist Americans to save our country." We lived in Saigon, in the south, and I was born in the early Seventies. My dad served in the army in the south – our ally was the United States. I spent my entire youth there, and I went to school there, first grade through twelfth. After I graduated from high school, I stayed there for four more years before I came to the United States.

When the war ended, it started a new chapter in our lives. To me, it was the darkest time for Vietnam. People blamed it on the war, but I think it was the Communists who ruled my country. It was really, really bad over there when I was growing up. They used the Communist way to oppress everything.

All soldiers who served the Southern army, especially the officers and government functionaries, had to report to concentration camps, most of them deep in the malaria-infested jungle areas. They called them reeducation camps. Depending on their "crimes" and based on their rank, they served anywhere from a few weeks to twenty years.

Thousands of camp inmates died from lack of food, medicine, or clothing. Thousands committed suicide, some were secretly liquidated, and others perished through staged "accidents." Former officers were forced to deactivate minefields with their bare hands so the regime would not have to waste valuable bullets on them. After the officers had mostly been eliminated, the intellectuals – some 2,500 of them – were imprisoned in the re-education camps. Among them were journalists, authors, scholars, professors, student leaders, Western-educated technicians, and Third Force leaders.

They did a lot of awful things to us. They targeted whoever had any property, especially the bourgeoisie: "rich people," business owners, and property owners. They came into people's houses and seized everything: money, gold, diamonds, homes, and our land. They sent them to what they called the New Economy area, a concentration camp where people were forced to farm. In all, about 300,000 people were detained there. The living conditions in those areas were horrible. There was no electricity, no running water, no basic necessities. Most of those people had never seen the soil before, let alone know how to grow their own food.

The next blow was changing the currency, and the value of our money turned into nothing... useless. That was social justice for all: We were all equally poor, except for members of the Communist Party who just seized all our property!

That created a flood of people trying to flee the country in the late Seventies and early Eighties. I know a lot of people who sold everything they had, just to get into a little boat to cross the Pacific Ocean. If they were caught by the Viet Cong, they were shot at. The V.C. used AK-47s, and just fired into those little boats with women and children – they didn't care. If they caught you, they put you in prison or you were killed. Some of the refugees fled, and some of them died on the sea of starvation and dehydration. Some of them were picked up by big boats from the West, and got into refugee camps.

My best friend's uncle left in one of those boats, and they ran out of food. The pirates raped the women and took all their property. They were left with nothing to eat, and they starved – people started eating the dead. Oh yes... when people got to the refugee camp in Hong Kong, they started telling stories.

In 1989, my dad took my two brothers to run away. Most people run by the sea, but my dad and my brothers ran across the Cambodian border. They got into a refugee camp in Thailand, and were there for two years.

Life in the refugee camps wasn't very good, either. They lived off the charity of the Red Cross, and there was a lot of corruption there. My dad said that when they got their meals, if there were maggots on the chicken, they just washed it off and cooked it. And that's in the refugee camps run by the Red Cross. They went through a hard time, and then were transferred into the Philippines after two years in the camp. They finally made it to the States in 1991. It was a long journey.

To us, to come to America and experience freedom... we understand it's not free. There was a price. Why did people leave Vietnam? Because we lived in oppression over there. Up until this day, they are oppressed. They repress freedom, they repress freedom of speech.

I went through first grade through twelfth over there, and all they taught us was propaganda. Marxism, Leninism, and other propaganda about Communism being great. Property should be transferred to everybody. The rich are evil. All that Communist propaganda – we couldn't study anything else. The teachers in school don't get paid much, either. Everything's run by the state, so they didn't really teach very well.

I learned more than what was taught at school because my parents paid to let me take extra courses. I got to learn the real math, physics, and chemistry elsewhere... not in school.

School was only half a day. I went to school until noon, in time to clear the room for the second class.

The teachers taught extra hours at home, and collected money from the students. If you didn't take the extra classes, you wouldn't get good grades. There was corruption from the top to the bottom.

I knew we were taught propaganda all the time, because our parents lived in Saigon during the times of the Republic before the Communists took over. We lived with the Americans, so my parents taught us right and wrong. We learned everything at home, but at school, we had to sing their song to get a good grade. You're not allowed to express your own opinions at all. You had to comply with their doctrine. Everything we learned was only one side of the story. It was awful.

There's no real opportunity over there. We took exit exams to graduate from high school, and I had the highest grades in the whole school. Yet, I didn't get admitted to college. Everything is state-run. Everything is free; university is free, but you have to take the entrance exam. I didn't pass it. It's not that I *couldn't* pass it, because they don't really grade you. It doesn't matter whether you pass it or not – they already selected who's going to get in, but not based on grades. It's based on what your parents do. So, those kids whose parents were in the Communist Party got their priority to get in. My parents served in the old regime – I didn't have a chance.

I was fortunate my parents remembered what it was like before the Communists took over; they knew the other side of the story. Many parents from Saigon served the South and understood the difference. But the kids from the North have been fed Communist propaganda for generations. Just like the Chinese – they were Communists who have been brainwashed for decades. Many of them don't get it and live with that doctrine in the back of their minds. I've noticed that with a lot of my Chinese friends over here. They talk that way, but I can't blame them because that was how they were raised.

The Communists make sure you're immersed in that water. There is no other way. The longer you stay with them, the more you think like them. They closed off every kind of information when I lived there. It really was an Iron Curtain. No information in, no information out. I'm sure a lot of Americans don't know what's going on back there.

In the mid-Eighties, I went to Hue with my family, and my dad told me that he saw a U.S. Congressman there. In order to talk to him, he had to maneuver a lot to try to evade the "tails" that followed the Americans around.

Back in the Eighties, the only foreigners in the country were Russians. Talking to a foreigner, especially an English-speaking foreigner, was bad. When I say bad, I mean you could go to jail for that. They'd throw you in jail for any reason, or no reason at all. There are no lawyers the way we have them, no law school, no nothing. We used to say that they have jungle law – it's lawless.

I display the South Vietnam flag online. Over there, if you display that flag, you go to jail. If you wear the old South Vietnamese uniform in public, you go to jail. There's no freedom at all.

If we wanted to leave our city to visit my grandma, or go to another province, we had to get a permit to travel. Once we got to our destination, we were required to register with local authorities in order to stay there, even for a couple of days. There's no guidance for when we needed a permit, no idea what trips required them. It's just up to the local police, and they just try to get money from you. You want a permit? You give them some money, and you're fine. It's just corruption from top to bottom, everywhere, for everything.

All gatherings, even a birthday party or a family reunion, must be preapproved with a permit. In America, you don't think of a birthday party as representing the freedom to assemble. We have a few generations of Americans who have never wanted for anything, and never had their freedom threatened. I hope they don't take it for granted.

The health care system is full of corruption, too. The doctors don't make any money from their government positions, so they don't really care for their patients. The "wonderful" state-run health care is free for all. Anyone, even a child, can walk into a clinic and get an abortion, an IUD, no questions asked.

Human life is cheap. Corruption was everywhere. My brother fell off his bicycle and poked a hole in his ribcage near a "children's" hospital. There was blood everywhere. His friends took him there, and they turned him away because he wasn't a child – he was only fourteen! Another time, my other brother needed an emergency blood transfusion in the hospital, but they wouldn't do it because my parents didn't have the cash to pay for the blood. My aunt ran across the street and pawned her gold chain – she saved my brother's life!

There isn't much medicine around; it's mostly domestically made and useless. My grandparents from France used to send us medicine, which we turned around and sold. You could buy medicine from anybody. If you have a toothache, they'd just pull your tooth instead of fixing it. I have so many missing permanent teeth now. I have crowns and bridges all over my mouth because of that. They did nothing.

When my dad had some money, he took us to a dentist who worked from his kitchen. He worked for the government hospital and had his little private practice, but it wasn't legal. He gave us some fillings, and other stuff that they don't really do from the hospital. There was no anesthesia. You'd go there and they drilled your teeth – no numbing, nothing.

There was no advanced medicine, and conditions in the hospital were horrible. You've seen the footage from Cuba? The same thing. I heard that recently, it's nicer because they let people have private practices. So, people with money can afford to go to a private practice, and it's pretty decent. But there's still a gap – the rich get richer from the Communist Party, and the poor just stay poor.

I live in Virginia, and sometimes I go to D.C. for the Memorial Day weekend and see a lot of Vietnam Veterans riding their motorcycles. I know about the protest movements during the Vietnam War, and that the media decided it was a bad war, that we had no business trying to keep Communism from spreading. The U.S. forces withdrew. I know it pained so many who served, trying to keep the Communists from taking over. That turned the momentum back to the Communists. The Americans were winning, and they were ordered to lay their weapons down. They were ordered to stop fighting.

That is so wrong, how the protestors treated the veterans back then. They had no idea of the consequences of the U.S. withdrawing from Vietnam. It ruined a generation. They put those men who fought with the United States in jail in jungles, in forced labor camps. If the Southern army soldiers did or said something the Communists didn't like, they'd just shoot them. It's horrible, it's horrible. It changed them.

My best friend's dad came back from one of those camps, and now he's afraid of everything and everybody. He's in the U.S. now, but he can't get a job. He's just afraid.

I've heard that in those camps, if the prisoners needed surgery, they operated with a razor blade. It's very inhumane, but the West doesn't know anything about it. They wouldn't let you know. I think whenever somebody from the outside investigated, they staged the whole thing. Some of the guards pretended to be the prisoners; they looked healthier, because they were better fed. When you look at the real prisoners, you can tell that they were ill-treated. You can tell. That's why they have to stage stuff, and act like they were prisoners.

We lived in very poor conditions. Families got a food card to get rice or oats for free. They were supposed to last for the month, but only lasted about a week. There was no other way to put food on your table. I remember my three-year-old brother woke up crying one morning, and tried to drink hot water to calm his hunger, which obviously didn't work!

In the late 1970s, both of my parents worked for the government. All the companies and factories were state owned. All the workers were state unionized. My dad worked for the city's only TV station, and my mom worked for the local theater, reading the translation scripts for foreign movies. The only movies allowed were from their Communist allies: Russia, Poland, and Romania.

We were considered middle class, yet it was a real struggle to make a living for all of us. My dad sold cigarettes from a homemade wooden box during breaks at work. Whenever my parents weren't working, we sold cigarettes from a stand near our house. I spent many hours helping them, doing my homework there alongside the prostitutes on the sidewalk. When we were younger, my parents just locked us up inside the house when they went to work. We had the key but the lock was outside. There were no babysitters.

I had to do housework very young. By age eight I already went to the market daily to buy food because we had no refrigerator. I budgeted the food money, cooked, washed clothes by hand for the whole family, and took my brother to school and back using my mom's bike.

Later, I made some money for our family by making yogurt and putting it into little plastic bags; my mom froze them at the theater and sold them to moviegoers. I learned how to mend clothes at an early age. We only got new clothes once a year at Tet, the lunar New Year – everything had to be the best to bring a good year. Our typical meal included rice, vegetables, about three ounces of beef or pork, or two duck eggs for the whole family. We didn't try to keep our weight down – that was all we could afford.

They cut our electricity three or four days a week, and many nights I studied under the oil lamp. We had no TV during the day. TV was only broadcast a few hours a night and was state run. I spent most of my time reading books. I've read a spectrum of authors from all over the world.

They cut our water several days a week. You'd turn the tap on, and there was no water. There wasn't enough to go around, although Vietnam has wonderful resources. We have the most beautiful coast that runs the length of the country. We have the rain forest, the mountains... but no technology, provisions, or even the interest to make use of the resources.

Everything was so limited. It's the same concept – do to your ability, and earn as you need. As a result, nobody wanted to do anything! No one was allowed to do anything innovative anyway, because the government controlled every aspect of your life. Marxism doesn't work. It never works. It won't work. And we know that – we lived through that. That why I get so frustrated now to see the United States heading that way.

There's just no motivation with Marxism. Nobody wants to excel, because they know they wouldn't get anywhere. That's just what people on the left keep saying, how great it is to spread the wealth. Who's going to make the wealth to spread it? Nobody's interested in making wealth for everyone else. They know wealth wouldn't trickle down since it already flows into the pockets of the corrupt government.

When I hear Americans talk about redistributing wealth... those people, they are living on clouds. They just don't get it. They've lost their common sense. Everybody's going to end up equally miserable.

I arrived in the United States during the Rodney King riots in April 1992. One day after I came to the United States, I started working in my cousin's nail shop in Los Angeles. I took the bus to downtown L.A., and people were burning houses down – it really wasn't what I imagined before I came here.

My dad and my brothers had moved to Monterey Park, California, and when my mom and I moved there, all five of us lived in a one-bedroom apartment. I think they were on welfare for about three months, and then they found jobs– these small, skinny men delivered big pieces of furniture.

When my mom and I came, we had nothing. We were penniless. I learned how to do nails, and did that to put myself through school. It took me about six years to get my bachelor's degree because I moved from place to place and worked while going to school. I went to East L.A. Community College from 1993 to 1995, and moved to the East Coast right after that. I got my bachelor's degree in Management of Information Systems, and graduated with a 3.99 GPA, and then earned my master's degree after that, but I never took any government benefits, even for one day. I never relied on the system. At one point, I worked full time at the nail shop and went to school full time. I took about twenty credits, five or six classes, and made all A's.

I basically went to class and went to work. I didn't make any friends; I just focused. No parties, no vacations. We focused. We knew what it meant to have nothing. We knew where we came from. I took courses in business, economics, and accounting. When I came to Virginia, I bought and ran a small nail salon, and put myself through school. I work full-time and I still have the salon. It's small and I just employ family.

In Vietnam now, the social classes are still very far apart. One is very rich, and one is very poor. People from the Communist Party got richer and richer because they've got everybody's money from all the corruption. They're so rich they can send their kids over here and buy houses for them, paid in cash. They spend money like crazy. Most of the people are very, very poor. Some foreigners go over there and think, oh, that looks nice. But from the bottom, people still suffer. I don't think things will change there unless they change the regime – it's still Communist.

In 1954 in North Vietnam, the Communists started a movement called the Land Revolution to clear out the land owners. They got the kids to turn their parents in for "crimes." It was kind of like the Hitler Youth. They were accused of speaking against the Communists, of owning land and employing people. They were considered evil by the Communists. Those people got hanged. It's horrible.

Even during my time in Vietnam, I remember living in fear. We were afraid to say anything against the government. I think a lot of Vietnamese immigrants still have that mentality.

They're afraid of authority. They're afraid of the police. I even had that fear when I was in California. I got stopped by a cop, and I hadn't done anything wrong. It was just a routine stop and he let me go, but I had that feeling. I respect a lot of Vietnamese for speaking their minds against the government.

I think that people turning their backs on any kind of faith or spirituality has been part of the problem in the United States. It was difficult for us to pursue our religion in Vietnam, and any religious speaker who opposed the government was oppressed. In April 2007, Father Nguyen Van Ly was sentenced to eight years in prison for "spreading propaganda to oppose the socialist government of Vietnam." He was fighting for the freedom of religion, and he was arrested. The last time he was in court, it was ironic. At the trial, they were very quick to cover his mouth with a hand. It's a famous picture. They covered his mouth as soon as he shouted, "Down with Communism!" Father Ly has been in prison for fourteen of the last twenty-four years for pursuing democracy and religious freedom for Vietnam.

In a lot of American schools, you can't express anything religious. I don't think some of these kids have any base, and they don't have the religion to rely on, to ground them. There are so many temptations, so much trouble out there.

In Vietnam, most of us are Buddhist, some are Baptist, and a large portion of the rest are Catholic, because of Father Alexander de Rhodes, a French Jesuit missionary. Father Rhodes wrote the first Vietnamese Catechism and published the first Portuguese-Latin-Vietnamese dictionary. This dictionary was later widely used widely by Vietnamese scholars to create the new Vietnamese writing system, using the Roman alphabet.

I don't really practice because we were discouraged from practicing our religion when the Communists were in charge. My father is Catholic, and took us to church when we were very little, but just stopped going after that. I think he went back when he fled the country for the refugee camp. My brothers were baptized, but I stayed behind with my mom. I wasn't formally baptized. I'm open to Christianity, and I would like my children to get into religion.

One of the really evil things about Communism is that they destroy people's faith. They believe in no deity, no faith. Their faith is Communism. You can't have both. They don't encourage people to have religion because they believe they *are* a religion. They try to get people to worship Communism. In January 2010, at Dong Chiem, North Vietnam, they sent the police and even the army to besiege that little village. They even beat children and old people who dared to peacefully protest the destruction of the cross in the parish cemetery.

When I was in college in California, my English 101 teacher introduced us to Larry King and Rush Limbaugh to compare and contrast. I had no political preference then, and I had no idea about conservatism, or Democrats or Republicans. I listened to both, and I loved Rush Limbaugh! It was a natural inclination. I still listen to him. I think he's very smart.

When I got too busy with school, I didn't listen to talk radio much. When my dad moved to Virginia, he said, "I listen to the Rush Limbaugh show, the guy you used to like." So I started listening to him again. My dad was a long-time Democrat voter, and ever since he came over here, he listened to me, changed his mind, and started voting Republican. I moved to Virginia in 1996, and my other family was in California. One by one, they have all come here.

People say conservatives are mean, but I don't see it. I was only one of a few conservatives at my previous workplace, and it was pretty rough. Some of my co-workers were just downright mean. Now I work with a lot of conservatives and watch conservative shows. I don't see any hate in Sean Hannity or Glenn Beck.

Some people I know on the left are cold and think mostly of themselves. After *Time* magazine ran a cover story about Glenn Beck, a young woman wrote a letter to the editor in October 2009 that ended with, "Grandma, step aside. We want our health care and we want it now!" How do you expect your kids to respect you if you don't respect your grandparents? That's what the Communists did – they told the kids to turn on your parents. So, they reported their parents. I don't ever want to see that here.

Now I see echoes of what I experienced in Vietnam. I think the administration goes in that direction, too, by targeting Fox, Rush, Hannity, and Glenn Beck. It's scary. Have you ever seen any administration go after a news station, a talk show host? It's unthinkable that the government would say Fox News was not a real news organization. That shocked me. I was so happy to see Jake Tapper and other reporters say that if Fox isn't going to be in the press pool, we're not going to be, either. It was unthinkable, what happened. That increased the number of Fox's viewers, and I don't think the administration is done yet.

When I took my five-year-old son to summer day care in 2009, he said, "Mommy, you have to give Obama a chance!"

I asked him, "Where did you get this?"

"My teacher said that."

Uh-oh! They're not supposed to talk politics to my son! So I had a little talk with the teacher and told her our point of view. When I heard about the Obama talking points for the students for the first day of school, that worried me. I don't care about him talking to the kids. I *do* care about the questions. I emailed the principal and said that I don't believe in any propaganda. If you participate in this event, please call me or my husband and we'll pick our kids up.

Thankfully, his school didn't participate in that. The original questions for the high school students – "What can you do to help the president?" – that's not right. They're supposed to help the country, not one man. And those airhead actors in that video, saying they would serve the president. We don't serve politicians – they serve us!

So many people don't understand basic economics, and that you don't get extra money just by printing it. Like that lady said, Obama got the money from his stash?! It's not good for them; it's not empowering them. It's going to enslave them, because they rely on the government and not themselves. They won't move up. They're going to stay down.

My husband is an American police officer. He sees the programs, the "free money" is hurting them. It keeps them down there forever. He doesn't like this at all.

I don't think Obama's intention is to destroy our country's foundation. I think it's ignorance. He's probably from that environment, that radical left environment where people are living in fantasyland, and not in touch with reality. The same people who think that Communism is good... I would invite them to go live in Vietnam for a year. I think it's naïve. I don't think he would intentionally do harm, but he is doing harm without knowing it.

I once worked with people who believed these arguments. I didn't want to argue with them, but I told them that they didn't know what they were talking about. They kept saying that Bush was corrupt. I don't agree. I told them they didn't know *anything* about corruption or Communism.

We have a big Army base nearby. My work now is to support the Army training. I feel more comfortable, better than my last job. I feel like my work is worth doing and that I'm on the right course, helping the soldiers. I'm on their side. It's nice to give back, besides making a living.

I still have hope – real hope – that the American people will wake up one day. They woke up here in Virginia and New Jersey. After the election, I told my husband, *that* is change, real change. Americans changed their minds. I do have faith in American business. I hope they will turn around.

The average American can turn this around by staying up to date on the issues. So much is going on, very quickly, and a lot of Americans don't keep up with the current issues. They don't pay attention to politics. Just stay updated, keep calling your representatives, talk to people, and vote.

To this day, many Vietnamese lawyers, writers, and reporters are still in jail for telling the truth or publicly expressing their opposition to the government. I love this country. There's no place like it. Americans, appreciate and protect your true freedom!

Cindy Nguyen (right) and her cousin in South Vietnam.
(Photo: Courtesy Cindy Nguyen)

Seven

CUBA

"The mental effect on the people after the Revolution was despair. Being controlled, that they realized that they can't fight back any more."

John's parents on a country road near Camagüey, about a week before leaving Cuba, October 1962.

Cuba

CHRISTOPHER COLUMBUS HAPPENED UPON CUBA during his journey to the New World in 1492, and christened it "Juana" while claiming the land mass for Spain. In 1508, explorer Sebastien de Ocampo circumnavigated Cuba, proving it was an island. Columbus' son Diego was appointed governor of Cuba by Spain's King Ferdinand in 1509, thus beginning four centuries of Spanish Rule.

Slavery was introduced in 1513, as the dwindling numbers of indigenous peoples were not deemed strong enough for the demands of hard physical agricultural work and mining. During the next three hundred years, Cuba's sugar, tobacco, and coffee exports became famous worldwide, with the United States becoming the chief buyer in the early 1800s.

Throughout the 19th century, various Cuban factions engaged in numerous skirmishes with Spanish troops, fighting for true national independence. Finally, in 1897, a new Cuban government was elected but was unrecognized by U.S. President William McKinley. U.S. relations with Spain became strained with the explosion of the USS Maine in Havana's harbor in February 1898, leading to the Spanish-American War. Five months later, U.S. naval forces defeated the Spanish fleet in Manila Bay, Philippines, ending Spanish rule of several possessions. In December, Spain formally ceded control of Cuba, Puerto Rico, the Philippines, and Guam to the U.S. with the Treaty of Paris. However, the Cubans were not represented or consulted on this matter, and their quest for independence continued into the 20th century.

In June of 1901, the Cuban Constitutional Conventional finally accepted the Platt Amendment after a great deal of contention, which granted very favorable benefits to the U.S. government and commercial interests in Cuban affairs. In May 1902, the U.S. flag came down and the Cuban flag was finally allowed to fly over Havana under newly elected president Estrada Palma.

However, many Cubans resented any foreign presence at all in their homeland, and regarded the activities of U.S. and Spanish interests as *de facto* occupation. Cuban rebels voiced their displeasure with the attack of an army barracks in February of 1906, and by September, controlled most of the island. Fearing an outbreak of total anarchy that would also jeopardize U.S. interests, President Theodore Roosevelt installed the second provisional government in Cuba after Palma and his cabinet tendered their resignations. This involvement ended in January of 1909, and José Miguel Gómez was elected as the new Cuban president; he was replaced in 1913 by Mario Menocal for two terms.

The meteoric rise and crash of sugar prices in 1920 created universal economic concern in Cuba, and in 1925, the Cuban Communist Party was founded by two labor and student organizers. The Wall Street crash of 1929 created the worst economic crisis in Cuba's history, with sugar selling for a mere 0.57 cents per pound (from a high of 20.31 cents per pound in 1920).

For the next decade, Cuba endured general strikes, economic stress, and increased influence from the Communist Party. The Platt Amendment was nullified, the exception being a single U.S. military base at Guantanamo Bay. Fulgencio Batista was elected president in 1940, and legalized Cuba's Communist Party in 1943. The Cuban People's Party was formed in 1947, and was later known as the Orthodox Party. Batista ran for a second presidential term in 1952, polling a distant third in the three-way race. On March 10, 1952, he staged a coup, ousting incumbent president Carlos Prío Socarrás months before the June election. He rejected the prior administration's progressive stance and concentrated on amassing wealth and social prestige.

Fidel Castro unsuccessfully ran for Cuban Congress as a member of the Orthodox Party in 1952, and was arrested in 1953 after leading a revolt against the army barracks. He was sentenced to fifteen years in prison after his trial in October. Following an island-wide campaign in 1954 led by Communists calling for Castro's release from prison, he was released in 1955 as part of a general amnesty. Castro left Cuba for Mexico, and returned the next year to join rebels to plan the overthrow of the Batista administration.

In 1957, Castro and the rebels were interviewed by a sympathetic *New York Times* reporter, and then by a journalist from CBS television. The resulting film aired in May, followed by the rebels' release of the "Manifesto of the Sierra Maestra" in July, calling for all Cubans to form a civic revolutionary front. Ernesto "Ché" Guevara was promoted to Commander by Castro shortly thereafter.

The rebels made steady progress through 1958, taking town after town throughout Cuba. The U.S. refused to send military to help the Batista regime, as it was "unthinkable" that the rebels would succeed.

On January 1, 1959, Castro's revolutionary forces took control of Havana.

John B.

*"The regime picked an indigent family and moved them
into our house. Even if we wanted to come back,
we'd have nothing to come back to."*

MY PARENTS LIVED IN HAVANA when I was born in 1947 and
lived there until 1952. My dad had a machine business and a
mill that prepared cattle and chicken feed. It was quite profit-
able, because there were a lot of farms with a lot of cattle to
feed. Business was growing. It was a very vibrant city, very
cosmopolitan – you'd see people from all over the world.

My mother's family had a tractor agency in the eastern
province of Camagüey. When my grandparents died, my dad
moved us there so we could manage the business, which was
going very well. I'm an only child, so my cousins were fairly
close to me. We were an upper middle-class family, but not
rich. We had a house and servants – pretty much everybody
in Cuba had servants. Mom didn't work – she was a homemaker. We had a maid who came in to do laundry twice a
week, a live-in cook, and someone who cleaned the house
every morning and left.

Cuba was a very vibrant country then, very beautiful, very
green. There was an abundance of everything. Nobody went
hungry. No matter what your economic level, there was always a way to exist. Very few people asked for charity like the
homeless here in America. But if you wanted to work, there
was work to be done.

The constitutional government of Cuba was established in 1902, when it became a republic. There's a mindset endemic to Latin America that the leaders are never happy with what they have. They always want more; they always want to be *the* one in charge, so you always have coups. An official will get elected and three years into his four-year term, another guy says, Hey, I don't like the way you're doing it, so I'll kick you out, and I'll get myself in. And then he's in for a few years until somebody else kicks him out, and eventually they get back to another election. They establish another constitution, and then off they go for a few more years until it happens all over again. That set the stage for the Revolution.

In 1952, about the time we moved to Camagüey, Batista took power for a second time by overthrowing President Carlos Prío Socarrás, and he became a dictator. President Prío was a socialist, and he was taking the country in a direction that Batista didn't want. That set the stage for the coup. Otherwise, if you didn't do anything illegal against the government, you were pretty much left alone. There was no persecution or censorship. People were left alone to prosper and our business prospered. We did business with everyone from the little guy who had twenty acres, to the guy who had three thousand acres. We knew all levels of the farming society.

Cubans were very open. I remember the *guajiros,* or the small farm owners. Our whole family would take our Jeep on a Sunday to visit them. They might have bought a tractor the year before, and we'd go see if they needed any help with it. Nine times out of ten, my dad spent half the day fixing something for them for free. So, I learned how to fix tractors at an early age, and how to drive Jeeps and combines and everything. That's where I got my mechanical background.

Often, when people saw us coming through the gate, they'd send a kid out to grab a pig or a chicken, kill it and prepare lunch for us. That's how open they were. Some of these people were poor, and that was the only pig they had. My dad said, "No, no, don't do that. We'll come back, we'll come back." But that's what they wanted to do because of how they felt for us. That was the environment there.

I went to a private school because we had the means to, and because my cousins and all my friends went there. There was no animosity from the public school students against the kids who went to the private school. I never saw any discrimination in Cuba then. I didn't learn about segregation until I came to the U.S. It didn't exist over there. It was a very open society – half of our employees were black. Everybody sat at the same table for meals. Two of our maids were black, and we'd eat together. After our cook served dinner, she sat at our table with us. The cook might eat in the kitchen in other countries – there was none of that for us.

Then, of course, the Revolution came in 1959. I was about eleven years old, so I was very aware of what was going on. There was an immediate day-to-night change. All the wealthy people immediately left. My dad saw it coming – he knew of Fidel before the Revolution.

My dad's cousin ran the cafeteria concession at the University of Havana in the late Forties and early Fifties, and they would meet for lunch there. He kept seeing this one man at a desk in the corner of the cafeteria, and people streamed in to talk with him. My dad asked, "Hey, who was that man?"

My cousin said, "I don't know, some rabble-rouser organizer, Fidel Castro." He was a rich boy; his parents were very wealthy plantation owners in the eastern part of the island. He wasn't a downtrodden working-class peasant who rose up against the elites. He was an ultraliberal from wealth. He was always rabble-rousing in there, and always agitating for something. My dad's cousin said that he hung out with a bunch of avowed Communists... Marxists. He kept books by Lenin and Trotsky on the desk. He read all of them and gave lectures.

My dad said he was someone to watch. Throughout the Revolution, we knew who was in charge and my dad said, "You know, I really don't trust this son of a bitch." But Castro kept saying, Oh no, I'm not a Communist, I'm not a socialist. I'm just here to liberate the people from this dictatorship.

Since January 1, 1959, when we heard that Batista had left and Russia had prevailed, my dad said, "We're screwed." Then he told me, "I have confidence that the U.S. is not going to allow a Communist regime so close to its borders. We don't think it's going to happen."

My uncle was older and richer; three weeks after the Revolution, he packed up his family and sent them out of Cuba. He followed them a few weeks later – he just took all his money and left. My uncle said, "I'm done here. We're screwed."

My dad told him, "Nothing will happen. It will be reversed, trust me. The Americans will never allow this to happen."

Eisenhower was in office at the time, and then Kennedy was elected in 1960. In his Bay of Pigs invasion speech in April 1961, Kennedy said, "Together we must build a hemisphere where freedom can flourish; and where any free nation under outside attack of any kind can be assured that all of our resources stand ready to respond to any request for assistance." It was just posturing. Obviously, nothing really happened. That was one of the reasons we didn't leave Cuba in 1959.

There wasn't really any class warfare before Castro. Castro promulgated class warfare as a wedge once he took power, and to be able to say, "We're going to give all the poor people money, and redistribute the wealth." When I heard Obama say it was good to "spread the wealth around" during his campaign, I immediately flashed back to that.

In Cuba, a lot of the larger farms had employees. In the 1800s, the owners told the workers, "If you work for me, you can live on my land. I'll give you ten acres to build your own home for your family, and you work for me. If you want, you can eventually buy the ten acres from me." People worked for the large farm or ranch for ten or fifteen years, and then bought their ten acres.

Over the next sixty years, one huge ranch might be split into a group of smaller ranches – a patchwork of ten- to fifteen-acre plots of land. If a small farmer became prosperous, he could buy his neighbor's land and have thirty acres. There was a myriad of small farms around, each with a tractor and a pair of oxen for plowing and pulling the sugar cane carts. Every farm produced crops for market.

One of the first things that Fidel did was take land from the big farms. If you had more than five thousand acres, it belonged to the government. They took the entire farm away, not the "extra" acres, and confiscated it for the government.

Castro always started with the bigger farms. In late 1959, they started a system called the Agrarian Reform – they took your land away and gave it to the little guys, since the Revolution was supposedly for the little guys. Then, they told the little guys, "Look, you've got fifteen, thirty acres. You may have your little tractor; you may have your sons working for you. You can't be very productive – obviously, you only have a little bit of land. Why don't you give us your land, and we'll add it to the big land, and then you'll *all* work it, as a cooperative." Works great on paper, right?

The farmer thinks, Well, before I had fifteen acres. Now I can be part of fifteen thousand acres. So a lot of them did just that. They just gave their little bit of land away, and went to live in the big house. That worked fine until they went to collect their first paycheck.

Before the Revolution, the Cuban man was very accustomed to dressing up on Sunday in his white linen suit, grabbing his little fighting cock under his arm, and heading for town to fight his rooster. He'd drink, spend his money, and come home. Now he goes to the store and asks for his money. The worker at the government store tells him, "No, we're going to give you a voucher for the general store. You can buy your food, your coffee, whatever you need from there." Fine, no problem.

So, the man may tell the store clerk, "Hey, I need a new white linen suit."

"You can't have one, unless you pay for it."

"Well, I don't have the money, but I want one."

"You can't have one. You can have a set of working clothes because you're a worker. You don't need a linen suit to work, so you can't have it." The idea of equality just went out the window. The idea of "We're going to do for you" turned into "We own you and we're going to screw you."

The people became very dissatisfied. The idea that a thousand people working fifteen thousand acres will all produce and divide it equally works great on paper, except there will always be lazy people. The workers started to think, "I work the same as my neighbor, and get the same as him. What happens if I only work half a day?" He gets the same as his neighbor, because nobody kept track of how much anybody worked.

So, the next guy says, "You're getting away with only half a day. I'm going to work half a day, too." The same thing happened: he got his equal share, and he only worked half. After a year, the system broke down because nobody was working, and everyone drew the same salary. That's the fallacy of the system – it doesn't work. You must have an incentive to do better than the next guy; in order to work more, you must have the incentive to earn more.

That was one of the major changes that caused the standard of living to decline. The other change occurred when they started a neighborhood watch program, which is a very insidious system. They hand-picked someone in the most fervent Communist families in every block or two, and deputized them to be the neighborhood watch. They usually lived in the home of someone who had left. The government confiscated that home, and they moved the Communist family into this house, so now they owned it. The house became the community home, and everyone gathered in their living room. They even got to issue the rationing cards for the neighborhood.

Food became scarce because the farms weren't producing. They exported a lot of food to Russia to pay for their military aid. All the beef, sugar, beans, rice, soy – everything – produced in Cuba was shipped to Russia. Consequently, we had a scarcity of food. By the time I left in 1962, we were rationed four ounces of beef per person, per week. That's a Quarter Pounder a week. You could get a quart of milk per person, per week, only if there were children in the house. If there were just adults, no milk. Rice: a couple of pounds a week. Fish: you can have all the fish you want, but you get tired of eating fish after a while. Poultry: that also disappeared.

Before the Revolution we were beginning to export beef, lard, and pork products. That disappeared because it all went to Russia, so there were no pigs. We had a few pigs on our farm, and we could share one with the family on the sly every once in a while. We were nourished, but many people didn't have that. We were able to get a couple of chickens and some eggs at the farm once a week.

You needed a ration card to buy your meager rations at the store. It was issued by the neighborhood watch committee, the Committee of the Defense of the Revolution. They decided what you could and could not eat. If you talked against the government, you didn't work. If you did something that displeased them, they withheld your ration card.

The militia could – and did – search your house at two o'clock in the morning, rough you up, and throw you in jail for a week or two. No charges were ever filed, and in the meantime your house was left open for anyone to help themselves to your property. When you came back, you'd better toe the line, or it would happen again. That was the repression of the regime – that's how they kept everybody in line.

Before the Revolution, there was no gun control in Cuba. It was easy to go hunting, and there were shooting clubs. I had a .22 rifle and learned how to use a shotgun when I was twelve years old. When I rode my horse on the farm, I had my .22 rifle in a scabbard. My cousins all had revolvers and pistols. You could wear a weapon in Cuba prior to the Revolution. After the Revolution they confiscated everything. First they asked people to turn them in voluntarily, because the Revolution needed weapons. Next, they searched our houses for them, and then took them away without any compensation.

If they caught you with a weapon, you'd go to jail. They searched our house one day, and my mom had my grandfather's single-shot, muzzle-loading flint-lock. They actually confiscated it, and threatened to jail her because of it. Now, what harm can you do with a two-hundred-year-old flintlock?

When my aunt was in her late fifties, she was jailed for six months because she was so outspoken. My older cousin was also in jail, because he was outspoken.

The other part of the repression was gasoline rationing. We were fortunate that we had gas pumps for our tractor business. We could only sell so many gallons of gas, and we had to get rationing cards – we could pour a couple of quarts of gasoline in a can, so we had some gas. But everything was rationed, and nothing was available the way it had been.

The rationing had a physical and mental effect on us. We were used to walking into a store and having our pick of any brand of, say, canned soup. And suddenly, we had only one brand, made in Czechoslovakia or Romania, and we had no idea what's inside it because the label's in another language. That's all you can have. You can imagine the psychological effect of not knowing what you're eating. I can't read the can, and I don't even know how to prepare it.

We used to go to the meat market and tell the butcher to give us three pounds of rump roast, a leg of pork, and three chickens, and now you can only get four ounces of whatever there is. You don't even know what kind of meat it is. We lived a block from the bakery in the old part of town, and about ten p.m., they'd pull out the first fresh batch of bread, and it smelled so good. The neighborhood kids would go over there, and they could buy the irregular bread real cheap.

Now you can't do that – you have to wait until the morning, and everybody has to get in line. They can only sell it during certain hours. So, you become very regimented. That's the whole purpose of the socialist/Communist system: You regiment the people so you can control them. It's very hard on such a system to provide an abundance of food.

I was young, so I adjusted. But I could see it in my parents and the older generation that there was a lot of anguish, a lot of depression. At that time, there wasn't a way to determine when somebody's depressed, but we'd hear that someone committed suicide because he couldn't cope with it any more.

It didn't happen overnight, like today you can buy anything you want at the store, and the next day the shelves are bare. It was a gradual diminishing of products and services. All the doctors left the country because they had the means; they were the first to be restricted regarding who they could treat. The dentists, optometrists, they all just left the country.

The mental effect on the people after the Revolution was despair. Being controlled, that they realized that they can't fight back any more. You've heard the analogy that when you drop a frog in a pot of boiling water, it'll hop out, but if you gradually warm the water, it'll sit there and happily parboil to death without making a noise. That's pretty much what happened, a gradual change over about a year, from spring of 1959 when things started to tighten up, until about 1960, when it really finally dawned on people how bad things were. Up to even the Bay of Pigs, my father kept saying, "No, the U.S. government will not allow this to stay. They'll come here and do something about it." It was during the Bay of Pigs that my father said, "We're thoroughly, completely screwed."

I was in Cuba during the Bay of Pigs, and for about a week beforehand, we listened to Voice of America, translated into Spanish. President Kennedy kept saying, "We're going to take care of this. We're not going to allow this to happen," and so on. There were other clandestine radio stations that broadcast out of the Keys and the Cayman Islands. The government did their best to block those transmissions by broadcasting their own transmissions at the same frequency.

Radio repairmen were ordered that if someone brought in a radio for repair that was capable of receiving shortwave, they must disable the shortwave capability. I was told this by a neighbor who was an amateur radio operator. He was my inspiration for getting into the electronics field; I spent a lot of time at his house before the Revolution when I was about nine. I used to listen to him talk to people around the world. I developed an aptitude for electronics, and he taught me all the basics. When my dad brought his broken radio there, this guy told him, "I'll tell you how to fix it. If you bring it to me, I have to disable the shortwave."

We listened to Voice of America and some of these other stations. They said the invasion was coming, and that we shouldn't despair. For a few days before that, there was a big frenzy throughout the island. They mobilized the army, the militia, from one end of the island to the other. Army trucks drove back and forth, and they asked people to volunteer to become soldiers and to repel the invasion. They knew for about a week before that something was coming. There's a saying in Spanish that a war that is announced is ineffective. You can't announce or threaten an invasion. You have to just do it quietly. That's why they were preparing for it.

There was a lot of hope and anticipation in the Cuban people that it would succeed. Armed groups were ready to create a second front in Cuba, should the invasion succeed. When the invasion first hit, there was panic. The Cuban Army was in a panic when they heard there were planes flying overhead, bombs falling, and boats offshore. The people were scared.

During the invasion, the soldiers with long guns and the tanks would shoot the submarines, and the submarines just lit them up with a searchlight; they all took off running. They weren't really that motivated, but they put up a front. The Cubans expected the U.S. Marines to come ashore. When the first wave of the Cubans came ashore, the militia actually ran. There were mass executions of those militia for about a week after the Bay of Pigs.

One of those families lived down the block from us – their son had volunteered and was in the company that ran. He was executed... shot. His family members said he died in battle. But we know – the family knows – that they put the whole company up against the wall and shot them because they deserted. When they saw the invasion was real, they took off. Once they realized there was no U.S. force coming behind it, Castro's men found their *cojones*, went back, and shot or captured the first wave that came ashore.

If the U.S. had sent at least a couple of troop ships, and said, "We're coming ashore," they would have succeeded. The people who started the Second Front in the Cuban mountains were rounded up and shot. There were thousands that wouldn't have died. That was never publicized in the U.S. mass media, but if Kennedy supported the invasion with U.S. troops, we would have come very close to ending the Cuban Revolution. The Cuban army was *not* mentally prepared to fight U.S. troops. They would have surrendered *en masse*. It would have ended right there.

Right after that, Castro went crying to Khrushchev, and Khrushchev sent the missiles. I remember seeing the missiles being driven throughout the island. They came in the middle of the night on the main highway that goes through the center of the island, from east to west. Our agency was located right on this highway; my father and I were there late one night doing inventory, and we heard rumbling. We looked out the window, and saw a semi truck with long tubes on the back. They were support vehicles. So, the missiles were already there by July 1962.

Cubans had a lot of hope that it would succeed; after that, there was an even deeper despair. Until the Bay of Pigs, we thought, "We really, truly have hope." Afterwards, the people resigned themselves: We're done for, and nobody's coming to our rescue. We're going to die. We would either toe the line or die. That's when my dad decided we would finally leave. And it was almost too late for us.

For us to leave, a relative in the U.S. had to sponsor us. You couldn't just come in as a refugee, so my uncle in New York agreed to sponsor us. He sent us a U.S. money order to buy the tickets. You had to buy your ticket from Pan Am Airlines in Havana using U.S. dollars. The problem was, there were no U.S. dollars in Cuba because they had all been confiscated.

Cuba became a cash society towards the end of 1959. People took all their money out of the banks, and anyone who worked was paid in cash; you could buy goods on the black market with Cuban cash. In 1960, they changed the currency. One morning, the blue bills weren't good any more, and you had to buy the red bills. The round coins were no good any more – you had to use the new coins . All the currency was changed. Whatever money you had was worthless.

You could change only a certain amount per person at the bank. If your money was in a bank account, it was okay and was automatically converted. You'd show your I.D. card at the bank and exchange up to 200 pesos of Cuban currency per person for the new currency. They also marked your I.D. card that you had changed the money, so you couldn't do it a second time. That was it. If you had more than 200 pesos, you could use it to light up your cigar. Some people with more than 200 pesos made private deals to exchange the money. If you had U.S. dollars in your bank account, they were converted to pesos, and you couldn't get any dollars.

Once we had the plane tickets, we had to get a Cuban passport, about a six-month process. We eventually got the passports, and then we needed exit visas. Remember the movie "Casablanca"? The exit visa is very valuable; how much you had in your house dictated whether you got your exit visa.

When you applied for the exit visa, they sent somebody to inventory everything in your house. They counted your chairs, your silverware, plates, dishes, pots and pans... even your clothing: shirts, pants, underwear, socks. These people spent close to twelve hours in your house, inventorying and marking everything. They made a list and left.

Five months later, we got another notice that they were coming to inventory our house again. It was a telltale sign that we were getting ready to leave; they have to come back and check against the original inventory. There was a knock at the door about two o'clock in the morning. "We're going to inventory your house, and you have to leave the house and stay out." By that time, we no longer had our maid, because it was illegal to have a servant. It was just my parents and me.

They finished the inventory about three o'clock the next afternoon, and handed us the exit visas. They said, "There's the door, leave." You were only allowed thirty-five pounds of clothing and personal effects to take with you, including the suitcase. We had already bought the duffle bag, which was nicknamed *Gusano*, or "worm." That's what Fidel called people who left Cuba. It was already packed, and was exempted from the inventory. We had to buy new stuff to take with us – we had to leave the other stuff behind.

We parked the car in the carport and left the keys in the car. We had to call a taxi to take us to the Havana airport. We had forty-eight hours to leave the country. There were no buses. If you wanted to take a bus, you had to buy a ticket weeks in advance. We drove all through the night, and got to my aunt's house in Havana in the morning. When we got there, we had to run around some more to get the last of the paperwork and make sure it was correct.

We hadn't even arrived before our house was emptied and a new family moved in. The regime picked an indigent family and moved them into our house. Even if we wanted to come back, we'd have nothing to come back to. They took our car and put it into the police motor pool. It was done. There was no coming back. We went through the rest of the paperwork, got the visa verified, and went to the airport.

There were two daily flights out of Havana – one in the morning, one in the afternoon, with no flights on Saturday or Sunday. We were scheduled for a Friday morning flight on October 19th. When we got there, somebody had been left behind from the day before, so they took one of our seats on the morning flight. We were rescheduled for the afternoon flight. We had to arrive at the airport at four in the morning, and were put in isolation in a glass-walled room. They took our bags and searched them. They ripped open the seams to make sure we weren't taking any jewelry or gold. We could take a Russian watch, but no photographs, no documents, nothing.

We were isolated in the room and physically searched. They wanted to be sure we hadn't swallowed anything, then we had to go to the bathroom. We were there from four in the morning until flight time. If they suspected something, then they would X-ray you. Fortunately, they didn't suspect us, so we just sat there and went to the bathroom a few times.

We finally got on the two o'clock flight. The blockade was declared on Sunday. The morning flight on Monday the 22nd left about half full. The afternoon flight was sent out empty, and that was the end of the flights. We took the next to last flight that left Cuba in '62. We made it out by the skin of our teeth. After that, there were no more flights out.

Two of my aunts were able to leave a year later, but they had to go to Spain first. After six months in Spain, they were

able to make it to the U.S. We had different types of visas –
only ours allowed us to go directly to the U.S.

The feeling in Cuba after 1962 was one of resignation, knowing they couldn't do anything. The feeling I get through the
letters from our family there is still one of resignation. They
do their best with what they've got. There is abject misery. I
see photographs of the town, and the houses haven't been
painted since the Sixties. There's no paint available. The
houses are in a state of disrepair. But there is cement available
for the government projects. They can build bridges, monu-
ments, big impressive buildings – but for the people to build
their houses, there's nothing. There's just abject poverty.

People are paid the equivalent of about ten dollars a
month. They justify the low salaries because, well, there's
nothing to buy. What do you need money for? They still have
the old refrigerators from the 1960s. They brought in a batch
of Chinese refrigerators, but they didn't last. They broke.
Every last one of them.

The latest thing was the Chinese rice cookers Fidel
brought in. They still work, but you can only eat so much rice.
The Chinese eat rice all the time, but Cubans don't traditionally eat that much of it. The Cuban diet originally was very
rich in beef, pork, fish, and poultry, because it was plentiful.
Cuba is a country where you could throw a seed on the
ground, and it grows. You didn't even have to till the ground –
it was very fertile land. Now, the land is almost like Haiti.
They stripped of it the old plants, and now even the wild
fruits are gone. People are eating anything they can find.

There are very few dogs in Cuba, not because they're eating them – it's because there is nothing to feed the dogs. You may have a cat because it can catch rodents. There's a cat-sized rodent in Cuba called a *jutia*, similar to a nutria. People used to a joke that when folks were really poor, that's what they ate. Well, now that's become a delicacy in Cuba, if you can find them. So, that's the state of things. People will resort to eating whatever protein they can get.

One thing that Cuba can trade in is people, and they figure they can teach almost anyone to be a doctor if they have a halfway decent memory. They're taught by rote, so the universities crank out doctors by the dozens. Bolivia's university has very high standards, and graduate only the people who can really make it. Fidel tells Bolivia, "You don't have enough doctors, because they couldn't graduate from the university. We'll send you doctors for free." They are probably no more qualified than your average paramedic in the U.S. Fidel tells his brand new doctors that as payment for their free medical schooling, they will now go to Bolivia for two years, or they have to practice in Africa for three years. The free education is far from free. You pay for it one way or another.

My cousin is a dentist, and also became a professor of dentistry to adapt to the new regime. We had to send him materials to help fix a patient's teeth. He also needed eyeglasses, but couldn't get any in Cuba. My cousin sent him a set of drugstore reading glasses from Canada. So, that's how great Michael Moore's example of the Cuban health system was.

Any Communist regime must put up a good front. What Michael Moore was shown for his health care movie was a Potemkin Village, a fake. The true reality of Cuba is that there is some medicine. The hospitals don't have mattresses or bed sheets – patients have to bring their own. There's no food in the hospitals. The patient's family has to bring their own food, and they have to buy their medicines. Michael Moore painted a very, very pretty picture of something that is very, very ugly.

A very simple contrast can describe Cuba. Think of Beverly Hills, and think of Haiti before the earthquake. That's the difference. Cuba wasn't a First World country, but it was on its way there, and now it's lower than a Third World country.

I'm an American by choice. There might have been a time when I could have said, I don't like it here – I'm going to go to Spain or Puerto Rico or Brazil. But I chose to stay here, because this country is, in my opinion, the best country in the world. It has its faults, but there is no better place in the world. Americans by birth didn't have a choice about their citizenship. But I did, and I chose to be an American.

This country had so many opportunities when I came here in the Sixties. If you worked, you could make of yourself whatever you wanted. When we arrived in Miami in 1962, we had thirty-five pounds of clothing, and nothing else. No money. No property. We had some family, and were fortunate to secure a one-way plane ticket to Los Angeles, where a local church set us up with an apartment. One of the parishioners helped my dad get a job. Dad was a mechanical engineer, and worked as a mechanic because he was in his late fifties and didn't have the language fluency. It was decent, hard work, especially for an older man. My mother had never worked a day in her life. She didn't have to. She ended up doing laundry and ironing for people at home.

I was lucky to be given the last semester of my freshman year at a private high school in Los Angeles. After that, I worked at that school every summer, saved my money, and worked after school to pay the tuition. I never went to a public school in the U.S. This country gave me the choice to do that and didn't dictate what I had to do.

I went to school, worked, and progressed through life to where I was secure. I'm retired now, but I did reasonably well. This country allows us to do that. There were no restrictions, no class systems. I never felt I was discriminated against by anyone because of how I looked or spoke. Nobody gave me anything special, nor did they take anything away from me. I competed on my own merit, and did everything on my own.

I believe the slide into socialism that started in the Sixties is destroying this country, especially from quotas and political correctness. That's exactly what the Communist system does: It glorifies mediocrity. If you allow someone to get into college with a 2.5 GPA because of their ethnic group, and you deny someone else with a 3.5 GPA, something's wrong. The class warfare industry is cranking all the time.

The Cuban government used to control the people by rationing food and energy. You cannot ration food in the U.S. It's impossible. It would take many years to destroy the food industry in this country to the point where you could ration food. Cuba exported all its beef, vegetables, and sugar to Russia in order to make revenue. They used that scarcity to control the people. When you only get a quarter pound of meat a week by the good graces of the block watchers, and no milk, you become weak. In a sense, rationing was a weapon.

Progressives use conservation as a way to control resources and the people. They say it's better to have *some* rather than *none*. That's not the point. If we pay for it, we should be able to use it when *we* need to, not when the government tells us we can. Cuba brought in diesel generators from China in around 2005. They weren't big enough, so they had to install hundreds of them all over the city in mini-substations. Of course, when they ran out of fuel, that whole section of the city went dark. They had destroyed the major power plants. They had a *huge* electrical infrastructure with multiple power plants. They weren't getting oil from Russia any more. They had a little bit of coal, but they mismanaged it.

The problem with a Communist government is that you have one source of everything. Only one. You have no competition. If you have no competition, you have no improvement. Government mandates don't improve products – competition does. If you have one car manufacturer, why should they improve it? You're going to sell that car regardless because you're a sole source. Look at Russia: they used to make the ZIL limousines. The vehicles they made in the 1960s looked like a 1950 Cadillac. In the 1970s, they still looked like a 1950 Cadillac, because there was no incentive to improve them.

In the United States, limousines get improved every year. They change their design, they become more comfortable, efficient, and cleaner burning. When you pay people to improve the efficiency of a car, people will want to buy it. You don't need government with a whip to force you to buy the hybrid. You buy the hybrid because you want to.

I'm a very strong supporter of the Second Amendment. The whole point of the Second Amendment is for the people to protect themselves from the government, not from each other. The government doesn't understand that.

What do I like about this country? The opportunities are still there, if you can find them. They're not as plentiful as they used to be, because there are too many special interests that want their own people to get these opportunities.

The parallels I see between Cuba in 1959 and America today is that in one year, our government put in practice almost everything that Fidel did by force. Instead of doing it at the point of a gun, they're doing through laws and executive orders. It's what the Founding Fathers wanted to avoid with the staggered elections between the House, the Senate, and the Presidency. But now, there's a three-way majority. So you can almost have a monarchy... a dictatorship, if you will.

The other problem is that the mainstream media does not tell the public everything that's going on. They're so biased, so arrogant, and they leave so much out. Fox News reported pretty comprehensively about Scott Brown's election in Massachusetts. It seemed like the mainstream media's approach was, "By the way, there was an election in Massachusetts. We *think* the Republican won. Now, to other news..." They didn't go into the ramifications, that in a state where the Kennedys *owned* the seat of power, a Republican won it. A reporter asked Brown why he thought he was entitled to Ted Kennedy's seat, and Brown said, "It's not Kennedy's seat – it's the people's seat." The arrogance is still there. It's part of a radical agenda. So what can people do?

I see this administration as arrogant. They think they know better than us. Be quiet, we know what's best for you. That's exactly what the Cuban government told us. We know how to run your lives for you. You don't have a say anymore in your lives. That's the parallel with Cuba.

The difference is, this is a larger country, both in size and population. Cuba is a very small country, so it's easier to deal with. Also, there's a large number of ethnic groups in the U.S., and it's not so easy to control a country like that.

There's a large segment of the population that's not engaged in the political dialogue. We used to call the Cuban Revolution the Toe Revolution. You didn't become agitated until somebody stepped on your toe. You see your neighbor's house taken away, well, it's his house. They're leaving me alone. You see the guy down the street taken away in shackles. Oh well – it's not me.

But the minute they take your house, take you away in shackles, then you get agitated, but by then it's too late. People have to be aware of what's going on in their lives. Our biggest problem is a lot of people don't give a rat's ass about what's going on with the government. As long as they aren't directly affected, they're not engaged. They don't care.

The people who attend the tea parties and town hall meetings aren't special interest groups or extremists – they're just people. They're just regular people who finally got their toes stepped on, or they saw their neighbors' toes stepped on. The administration said they didn't care what anybody has to say – they'll do what they want anyway, even if they go down in flames in the 2010 elections.

People have to become informed about the issues, and think about who will ultimately benefit by voting for a specific person or party. The other problem is I think many people vote emotionally. "My friend told me to vote for this person. I'm voting for this person because it's hip. I'm voting for this person because I don't like the other guy." Well, do you know *why* you don't like him? Tell me the issues, and look not just at the short-term gain, but what we're leaving our children and grandchildren. Are we saddling them with debt? Are we going to leave them a better nation?

It's important for us to safeguard our rights, and have the right to defend them against a person or a nation bent on hurting us. Look at the candidate – who were they ten years ago? Remember the old saying: Tell me who you associate with, and I'll tell you who you are.

When people in Cuba told my father, "Oh, Fidel Castro's not a Communist," he asked, "In a whorehouse, is the madam a virgin?" Tell me, if he is not a Communist, why does he have Ché Guevera? Fidel and his brother were Communists. They studied in Russia, and hung around other Communists. You tell me. "Oh, Fidel needs to hang around those guys for guidance." Guidance? And look at Obama's associations with Bill Ayers and Jeremiah Wright. He went to Wright's church for twenty years, but he never listened? He didn't hear?

The other problem is academia. I know an elementary school teacher who's told what to teach her students. She has her own conservative ideas, but can't say anything about them. They are inculcating the kids with liberal, progressive ideas, which the kids then bring home.

The Catholic school I went to in Cuba sent the priests and the brothers packing out of the country at the end of 1959; they were mostly Spaniards. From 1959 until I left, I was home schooled. The last generation raised before the Revolution wasn't indoctrinated. The first generation raised under the regime was inculcated in Communism from their early days in school. That's all they learned. I think that what goes on in the schools and the media may take the U.S. down that path.

People are competitive and innovative, especially young people. They see that it's not fair that if you work hard, somebody else gets part of what you earned when they did nothing. If you work for eight hours at ten dollars an hour, you make eighty dollars. The government taxes you twenty dollars, and then gives eighteen dollars of that to a guy who's on welfare, just sitting around doing nothing. So you say, wait a minute! Why is he getting eighteen of my dollars, when I busted my butt for eight hours a day, making the money?

I try to teach my grandkids conservative values. You work, and it's yours! What's considered conservative values used to just be American values. It's the way my family was in Cuba. I learned my work ethic in our family business. My uncle was the general manager, and everyone in the family earned a share of it. Everything else was put back into the business, so we got bigger each year, instead of giving it all away.

The parallel between the Cuban Revolution and what's happening now is one of subtleness, of size. In the Thirties, Forties, and Fifties, the socialists and Communists took over Cuba with bloodshed and shooting, and imposed their way of doing things. They have learned that doesn't really work.

They learned from the frog in the boiling water, and went to the warm water approach, and changed things a little bit at a time. They strip away your ability to make decisions for yourself, to control your own life. In Cuba, though, they took immediate control by force, at the point of a gun. They took your land away and forced you to work in a cooperative. We're taking your home away because you have a five-bedroom house, but only two people live there. We're moving three more people in there so they can use those rooms.

Here, it's all been done subtly. We're going to do this in the spirit of social justice because it's not right for you to have a five-bedroom house if there's only two people in your family. You should *allow* someone who's on welfare to move in. We're taking control of the banks, of the car companies, of the health care system. The end result is the same: social engineering, control of the people, and control of the economy.

The biggest parallel I see between Cuba and the Obama administration is the same mindset: The government knows best, and we're going to control everything for you.

Cuba controlled the population by curtailing people's ability to move freely from one town to another. They didn't allow you to have a vehicle in the interest of national security, because the invasion was coming from the Americans. Also, because of the Cuban government's ineptitude, there was no fuel, no transportation. The whole infrastructure broke down.

The indoctrination in the schools, especially the so-called green, environmental B.S. that's going on, tries to steer young people's minds. You have to follow Dear Leader's suggestions. In Cuba, it was the worship of Fidel Castro, and here, it is the worship of Obama. When I saw the YouTube clips showing the students singing odes to Obama, that raised a big flag with me. The students in Cuba's public schools said the Pioneer Pledge in Cuba: "I am a pioneer for Communism. We will be like Ché." Then they'd sing the *Internationale* song.

I think that in the U.S., political opinion should be learned at home, from the parents. The schools should be neutral, and teach history, civics, the structure of the government. Facts, not ideology. A lot of teachers in the U.S. teach ideology – that's social engineering. The teachers should *not* interject any sort of political opinion. Schools are a place to learn and prepare yourself for life, especially in a country as varied as the United States. Cuba was fairly homogeneous. Here, we have so many different cultures. Some parents don't take an active interest in what their children learn or monitor what their kids read online. So guess what happens? Academia preys upon them, and the children get molded.

Look at the Cuban people who were able to take their money out of Cuba – and a lot of us didn't – but we have prospered. We have made something of ourselves. In Miami, a lot of the professionals are Cubans. In Koreatown in Los Angeles, a man who was a dishwasher when he was a teenager now owns three restaurants. They work very hard and instill the same values in their children. Man is of two natures: very hard-working or very lazy, and then you have the middle that's mostly complacent. It's been made too easy for them with the social programs. Look at the Vietnamese community that re-built their neighborhood after Hurricane Katrina while so many others waited for FEMA trailers. And after the 1994 earthquake in Los Angeles, the immigrant communities banded together and helped each other.

When I first came to Los Angeles, our neighbors worked for the General Motors assembly plant in Van Nuys. Around 1964, there was a strike. Our neighbor told us they had to go on strike because they needed more money. My father told him, "You know, you are stupid."

The son asked, "What do you mean, we're stupid?"

Our neighbor was in his sixties. He was a farmer, came here from Mexico, met his wife, worked hard, and had the biggest home in the neighborhood that they built themselves. They bought brand-new Chevys every year at cost because of their union discount. He made $20 an hour, which was a lot of money back in 1964. My father continued, "What's going to happen now? You're going to demand $2 an hour more. GM will eventually to cave in to your demands, and they won't shortchange their stockholders, so they have to increase the profit by increasing the price of the car. Next year, that car that cost you $4,000 this year will cost you $6,000."

The son said, "Yeah, but I'll make more money by then."

"Okay, you can afford to pay $6,000, but the baker has to pay $2,000 more, and has to raise the price of bread because he has to make more money. The butcher needs to buy bread and sees it's fifteen cents more than last week. He has to raise the price of meat to afford this. He won't raise it just to meet the fifteen cents – he'll raise it more to make a profit. So everybody increases their prices. One guy raises his prices 10 percent, the next guy raises them 15 percent, and so on. That's how you get inflation. Eventually the price of everything goes up. The gas company has to pay their workers more money because food is more expensive, and they raise the price of gas. It's a vicious circle. Everything continues up, up, up."

At one point, it has to stop, to level everything out. Nixon tried that by freezing wages and prices, which backfired bigtime. He was trying to stop spiraling inflation. The unions and the greediness affected the prices of everything else.

In Cuba, there were labor unions prior to the Revolution, and they had negotiated forty hours of pay for thirty-two hours of work. They had paid medical and union workers had their own hospitals. In 1959, Castro abolished all labor unions. Obama was elected by making a lot of public promises to the labor unions. Politicians have always had their fingers in the unions' pockets, and the unions have subtly and behind the scenes supported socialistic, liberal politicians who influenced legislation that affects the unions.

For people to take a stand for their individual rights, they have to know the facts and become informed. Don't just listen to the mainstream media. Seek out multiple sources of news. I read a lot of international newspapers online, from Spain, Argentina, the *London Telegraph*, and so on. The same news is reported from different perspectives, and somewhere in between lies the truth. Unfortunately, many young people get their news from MSNBC, which is hardly objective, or from Saturday Night Live and the Comedy Channel.

Next, become involved. If you don't speak up, nobody knows that you're hurting. I have a pocketache – I'm bringing home less money than I did a year ago. How do I fix that? Maybe the solution is putting new people in Washington. Throw all of them out and start fresh again.

Talk to your neighbors – maybe they'll have the same ideas that you have. Talk with people in the supermarket. You can make an innocuous comment and see how they respond; you can see whether you can continue the conversation if they're of a similar mind. Maybe they know of an event that's coming up. Also, support the candidates who support smaller government to get us out of this mess.

The way this country is headed, to government dictating every part of your life, is not right. The survival of business is based on its performance. You have to bring your best game every time. Government sources don't need to do that.

People are slowly waking up to how blatant the administration has been. The Cuban Revolution was the revolution of the toe. Once the government steps on the toes of the mainstream media, the charade is all over. They probably know what's going on, but they're so damn cynical, they won't admit it. Once they admit it, it's all over.

It's slowly beginning to happen. More Democrats and some Republicans have decided not to run for re-election because they're going to get their butts kicked. It's better for them to retire than be voted out of office. If they retire as a congressman or senator, they can eventually run again. Once they're defeated, they have a harder road ahead of them.

Look at our country's name: United States. It's a collection of fifty individual states, the original premise of the formation of the original thirteen colonies. Each individual state is supposed to rule itself. The federal government's role is to provide an umbrella for the mutual aid of the states, with an army that could come to the aid of each individual state. Each state had its own militia at the beginning. Even during the Civil War, each state had its own army. The federal government said, if Ohio gets attacked, Illinois will come to its aid.

Each state was supposed to be responsible for its own economics; they were responsible for their own mail, employment, whatever. The only reason the federal government got involved in the early days was to regulate commerce so you could have a uniform set of tariffs across state lines.

That was why the Civil War was fought, not because of slavery. It was states' rights. The Tenth Amendment says:

"Those powers not specifically allocated to the federal government are reserved for the states." I know my Constitution. To me, that's the most important thing. If you don't know what your rights are, you can't defend them.

The United States is the prize that every radical wants to take, because they want to destroy it. We're the target. The left tries to discredit and insult whoever doesn't swallow what they say. People have to be strong in what they believe, and have the moral courage not to be discouraged, demoralized, or swayed by that sort of thing.

You can hear the same stories from any immigrant group. This has always been the greatest country in the world. It's the place everybody looks to, and says, this is where I want to go. It's the epitome of how we want to live. There's no freer place in the world than the United States.

The family tractor agency exhibit at a country fair in Camagüey, 1957. Notice the American flag on the roof.
(Photos: Courtesy John B.)

Eight

VENEZUELA

"And where do you go? Of all places,
this can't be happening to our country."

CARACAS
I V
C
E
N
T
E
N
A
R
I
O

1 5 6 7
1 9 6 7

Simón Bolívar, liberator of Venezuela, on his horse.

Venezuela

VENEZUELA, LITERALLY MEANING "LITTLE VENICE," first appeared on a map in 1500, coined by Spanish explorer Alonso de Ojeda while on a voyage with Amerigo Vespucci. Most likely the name was a sarcastic sailor joke, as the thatched huts built above the water on stilts by the indigenous population looked little like Italy's opulent Venice that the Europeans knew. Evidence shows that the region may have been inhabited by nomadic tribes for as much as 15,000 years prior to the arrival of Spanish explorers. The Timote-Culca tribes of the Andes even practiced advanced agriculture with irrigation and terracing, just prior to the "discovery" of Venezuela by Christopher Columbus in 1498.

When Ojeda saw locals adorned with gold jewelry, it gave rise to the legend of El Dorado (The Golden One), a land further inland with an abundance of gold. Soon, the shores of Venezuela and Colombia were teeming with Spanish explorers, and the colonization of the area came quickly.

The first Spanish settlement was Nueva Cadiz, established in 1500. The earliest town still in existence is Cumana, dating back to 1521, however, much of its early architecture has fallen to numerous earthquakes. Venezuela was ruled by Spain from Santo Domingo in what is now the Dominican Republic until 1717, when the viceroyalty of Nueva Granada was created in Bogotá and assumed governance.

The arrival of slaves from Africa to serve as a workforce diversified the population, and they soon became more numerous than the indigenous peoples. Gold mining kept Venezuela a valuable Spanish possession for three centuries, until Simon Bolívar joined a revolutionary independence movement started by Francisco de Miranda in 1806.

After several unsuccessful attempts and self-imposed exile to Colombia and Jamaica, Bolívar was able to raise a small army including British Legion veterans and horsemen from Los Llanos. With this force, Bolívar marched over the Andes and triumphed at the Battle of Boyaca, defeating the Spanish army and liberating Colombia in August 1819. Four months later, a new congress in Angostura proclaimed a new unified state called Gran Columbia, which included Columbia, Venezuela, and Ecuador, even though Venezuela and Ecuador were still under Spanish rule.

Venezuela finally achieved independence on June 24, 1824, when Bolívar's troops defeated the Spanish army at Carabobo. His forces continued to fight for South American independence after this victory, and by the end of the year, Ecuador, Peru, and Bolivia were also liberated. Today, Simon Bolívar is still considered one of the region's greatest heroes.

However, Bolívar soon saw the difficulty of governing the region. On his deathbed, he said, "This nation will fall inevitably into the hands of the unruly mob and then pass into the hands of almost indistinguishable petty tyrants." Gran Columbia only lasted a decade, and soon split into three separate countries.

For the next hundred years, Venezuela was ruled by a series of military dictators known as *caudillos*. Although this authoritarian rule brought some semblance of stability to the country, it was still plagued by civil wars and a border dispute with Guyana.

Defaulting on international loans during caudillo General Cipriano Castro's reign brought the navies of Great Britain, Italy, and Germany to Venezuela in 1902, and the blockade of Venezuelan seaports. Five more caudillos ruled Venezuela for the first half of the 20th century. The discovery of huge oil reserves starting in 1910 gave a huge boost to the economy, ultimately giving Venezuela the status of the world's largest petroleum exporter by 1920. However, very little if any of this newfound wealth trickled down to the average Venezuelan, who continued to live in poverty.

Venezuela was dependent on oil revenue, and other sources of income became neglected, including agriculture and manufacturing. Soon, Venezuela depended almost exclusively on imports from abroad, which was easier, but soon proved unsustainable.

Against a background of growing civil unrest, Rómulo Betancourt, the leader of the leftist *Acción Democrática* (AD), took control of the government in 1945. A new constitution was adopted in 1947, and in Venezuela's first democratic election, novelist Rómulo Gallegos became president.

Eight months later, a coup led by Venezuela's last dictator Colonel Marcos Pérez Jiménez overthrew the Gallegos administration. Although Pérez Jiménez plowed massive amounts of money into public works programs and built up Caracas, the economic and social discord remained.

When General Pérez Jiménez was overthrown in 1958 by a coalition of civilians and military officers, Venezuelans gained no small amount of civil liberties. To run the country, a power sharing agreement known as *Pacto de Punto Fijo* was reached between social democrats and Christian democrats.

In 1960, the Organization of Petroleum Exporting Countries (OPEC) was formed, including Iraq, Iran, Kuwait, and Venezuela. In 1961, a new Venezuelan constitution was adopted with 252 articles and a variety of social rights. Eight years later, the social democrats lost the presidential election but maintained a majority in the legislature. The judicial branch, however, became politicized and corrupt, with the courts' decisions heavily influenced by whomever had the deepest pockets.

In 1974, Venezuelan oil industries and the central bank were nationalized, setting the stage for steady nationalization of private assets by the government. In December 1982, army officer Hugo Chávez formed a secret group known as Bolívarian Revolutionary Movement 200 and vowed to change Venezuelan society.

After 1983, the Venezuelan Bolívar became massively devalued, and by 2000, the Bolívar had lost 16,185% to the dollar. In 1989, government-instituted reforms and increases in fuel costs resulted in the deaths of hundreds as extensive looting and rioting gripped the country.

Lt. Col. Hugo Chávez made good on his promise to transform the country in February 1992 and again in November, attempting successive coups on the presidential palace with fifteen thousand rebels. It failed, and dozens were left dead. (Chávez served only two years in prison after sentencing, was pardoned in December 1994, and was asked to leave the military.)

President Carlos Andrés Pérez was impeached in 1993 following a scandal involving the misuse of $17 million, and was replaced by Rafael Caldera. In 1994, Banco Latino failed, sparking a run on the currency. Bank Chairman Gomez Lopez fled the country just before a warrant for fraud could be served. In 1996, Pérez was found guilty on corruption charges and sentenced to twenty-eight months in prison.

By June 1996, Venezuelan assets under government control included mines, oil refineries, petrochemical, aluminum, and iron production facilities, beaches, ports, a large percentage of agriculture, prime real estate, 60 percent of banking, manufacturing, television, and radio. Most of these concerns ran at a deficit. In August, the general sales tax was raised 4% to 16.5%, after an inflation rate of 108% during the previous year.

In November 1998, a leftist coalition led by Hugo Chávez won a majority in Parliament. Corruption charges against Chávez were dropped due to senatorial immunity. The next month, Chávez won the presidential election, and planned to rewrite the constitution and replace the congress.

March of 1999 saw Congress approve a bill giving Chávez broad powers to manage the economy. It was vetoed by Chávez, who said it was not sweeping enough. Congress then gave Chávez the power to rule the economy by decree for six months. Chávez vowed to extend his presidential term from five to ten years. A constitutional assembly was scheduled to rewrite the nation's constitution. It was approved by voters, however, 60 percent of the voters abstained.

Throughout the remainder of 1999, the constitutional assembly declared a state of emergency and assumed sweeping powers. One hundred twenty-two judges were suspended on charges of corruption and incompetence, most of the functions of Congress were usurped, and an attempt was made to shut Congress down completely.

Chávez defeated Francisco Arias in the presidential election in July 2000, and Chávez's Fifth Republic Movement won nine of twenty-three governorships and a majority of the legislature. In August, Chávez met with Saddam Hussein, Libya's Moammar Khadafy, and Nigeria's President Olusegun Obasanjo to plan for upcoming oil talks. In October, Chávez met with Fidel Castro to discuss trading oil for Cuban products.

Thousands of Venezuelan businesses engaged in a twelve-hour work strike in December 2001 to protest Chávez's policies. At the end of the month, street vendors sold CDs of banging pots to drown out Chávez's long-winded speeches. His approval rating plummeted from 80 percent to 50 percent in just a few months.

On April 11, 2002, the military removed Chávez from power after an estimated 150,000 demonstrators marched on the presidential palace. Nineteen were killed. The next day, business association leader Pedro Estanga was installed as interim president. However, Chávez returned to power the following day after massive street protests in Caracas. Dozens were reported killed in the rioting and looting.

Many anti-Chávez demonstrations were held in 2002, some numbering over half a million participants. Some were countered by pro-Chávez demonstrations. In November, Chávez ordered the federal takeover of the Caracas police force. On December 20th, after a nineteen-day general strike, over a hundred thousand whistle-blowing protesters demanded Chávez's resignation.

In April of 2003, Chávez and his foes agreed to a referendum on his presidency. By December, more than 3.6 million petition signatures were collected, demanding the referendum for recall. Under advice from Castro, Chávez began to create emergency health, education, and welfare programs for the poor.

The Venezuelan supreme court ruled in March 2004 that the collected recall petition signatures were valid unless citizens disclaimed them. However, this ruling was overturned a week later by fellow justices. In July, Chávez granted citizenship to 216,000 immigrants under a fast-track nationalization plan.

Chávez survived August's recall election. The opposition claimed that many of the automated polling machines were programmed to limit the number of pro-recall votes cast, since the Chávez regime owned 28 percent of the software company co-owned by the firm that supplied the machines. The law that gave the government control over the content of radio and TV programming went into effect in December of 2004.

A massive agrarian reform program was launched in January 2005. Escorted by troops and police, government officials descended upon privately held ranches to determine whether they would be seized and carved up into smaller plots for redistribution to poor farmers. The government claimed the land was "underutilized." In August, Chávez granted land titles to six indigenous tribes in a public ceremony, claiming to reverse centuries of injustice.

During an oil trade meeting on September 6th, Chávez urged the nine attending Caribbean nations to consider Cuban-style socialism as an alternative to capitalism. On the 15th, Chávez used a global summit to chastise President George W. Bush for America's involvement in Iraq. The next day, Chávez was interviewed on ABC's *Nightline* program and claimed to have documentary evidence that the U.S. was planning a Venezuelan invasion.

On October 31st, a new Chávez-backed Latin American TV station went on the air as an alternative to corporate media outlets. In December, Chávez's governing party won full control of the 167-seat national assembly after the elections were boycotted by the opposition. Transparency International rated Venezuela 130th out of 159 in its annual corruption perception survey.

In January 2006, thirty-two private oil fields succumbed to state control, the result of a 2001 hydrocarbons law requiring oil production to be limited to companies with a government-owned majority. In April, Peru recalled its ambassador from Venezuela, citing Chávez's "persistent and flagrant interference" in its upcoming elections. In May, Nicaraguan Foreign Minister Caldera asked Chávez to stay out of his country's political affairs. Later that month, Chávez met with Khadafy in Tripoli to discuss "social programs based on oil revenues."

In July, Chávez met with Belarus president Alexander Lukashenko to sign seven agreements on military-technical cooperation, economic assistance, and a declaration pledging strategic partnership, as they shared similar anti-U.S. perspectives.

In September, Chávez referred to President Bush as "the devil" before the U.N. General Assembly. In October, thousands marched in support of Manuel Rosales, the main opposition presidential candidate who promised to undo what he called the ills of the Chávez regime.

In November, Chávez handed out $3 billion of early Christmas bonuses to public workers amid accusations of cynical vote buying just before elections. Chávez won reelection on December 3rd with 63 percent of the votes. A poll taken by Associated Press-Ipsos three weeks before the election revealed that 62 percent of those polled supported nationalizing companies when in the national interest. However, 84 percent of those asked opposed embracing a political system similar to Cuba's.

On December 18th, Chávez took the first step toward creating a single, pro-government party. He further announced plans to nationalize power and communications concerns, and freely stated that he had been a Communist since 2002.

During his inauguration speech on January 10, 2007, Chávez took the oath of office using Fidel Castro's famous exclamation, "Fatherland, socialism, or death – I swear it." He pledged to "build Venezuelan socialism" in his upcoming term. Eight days later, lawmakers gave initial approval to a bill granting Chávez the power to rule by decree for eighteen months to accelerate his sweeping changes. The bill was enacted on January 31st.

On May 1st, Venezuela's last privately held oil field was taken over by the Chávez regime. Two days later, Chávez threatened to take over the country's banks and the largest steel producer if they didn't contribute more to local industries. On May 19th, Chávez decided not to renew the broadcast license for RCTV, the most watched TV station, which was aligned with the Chávez opposition. Tens of thousands marched in protest. On May 28th, RCTV was replaced by a state-run channel, and tear gas and plastic bullets were used by police to quell the resulting protests. Although RCTV's programming returned to cable and satellite on July 16th, it faced an August 1st deadline to carry Chávez's speeches or be shut down entirely.

In late October and throughout November of 2007, many protests and scuffles were led by university students objecting to constitutional reforms allowing Chávez to seek re-election indefinitely. Some protests were attended by more than 200,000 people in Caracas, and soldiers used tear gas, plastic bullets, and water cannons to disperse the crowds. On December 2nd, voters narrowly rejected granting Chávez far-reaching new powers and ending term limits. It was Chávez's first electoral defeat ever.

On January 1, 2008, Venezuela created new currency by lopping off the last three zeros on all denominations in a bid to simplify transactions. Inflation had risen more than 22 percent in 2007. The National Assembly launched an investigation on March 26th after a congressman accused two of Chávez's brothers of acquiring seventeen ranches between them in just a few years. Eight days later, Chávez ordered the nationalization of the country's cement industry, citing the need to prevent exports needed for domestic construction and development.

February 15, 2009, saw the culmination of Chávez's continuing efforts to remain in power when he won a referendum to eliminate the twelve-year aggregate presidential term limit. He promised to remain in power for at least ten more years to enact his socialist revolution. Chávez's opponents asserted that his amassed concentration of power in all branches of government brought him much closer to being a socialist dictator, and that the elimination of term limits would "make him unstoppable."

Following the passage of the U.S.'s $787 billion stimulus spending package, Chávez exhorted President Obama to turn to socialism in a March 2009 statement on Venezuelan state television: "I recommend to Obama – they're criticizing him because they say he's moving towards socialism – come, Obama, ally with us on the path to socialism, it's the only road. .... Imagine a socialist revolution in the U.S. Nothing is impossible." Obama responded by stating it was not his intention to replace free-market capitalism with socialism, but that he wished to bolster the economy by reforming health care, energy policy, and education.

Several weeks later, Chávez marked the 199th Commemoration of the Independence Declaration of Venezuela by opining, "It would seem that the changes that started in Venezuela in the last decade of the 20th century have begun to reach North America." While Chávez is known for highly hyperbolic statements, he made no such predictions during President Bush's administration.

Chávez again devalued the currency in January 2010 to delay the contraction of Venezuela's economy, which shrank by 3 percent in 2009. This action, long part of the socialist economic toolbox, essentially doubled the prices of goods overnight, and Venezuelans reacted by panic buying and hoarding. Taking his cue from other socialist regimes, Chávez announced that businesses raising prices would be "confiscated" by the government: "Right now, there is absolutely no reason for anybody to be raising prices of absolutely anything. I want the National Guard on the streets with the people to fight against speculation. Publicly denounce the speculator, and we will intervene in any business of any size."

According to his opponents, Chávez already has far too much power, with the courts, the legislature, and the election council all under his influence.

Rebecca S.

"First he duped the people into thinking he was
their only hope, and now he won't leave.
Everything that Chávez does is an 'emergency'."

I LOVE THE UNITED STATES, and I've been here for thirty-three years, most of my life. I lived in Venezuela from the time I was born until I was ten. I remember a lot, and I keep in touch with part of my family, but I haven't been back since 1985.

My mom grew up in here in Miami, and then went off to college. She wanted to teach in Saudi Arabia or Venezuela because they had openings at the oil camps for American teachers. She chose Venezuela mostly because was closer to home. My grandparents weren't very pleased about her leaving, but that was her destiny. At the time, my father was doing graduate work at the university in Caracas. They had mutual friends, started dating, and then married.

I was born in Caracas, but my mom did a really smart thing: She went to the American consulate and declared me a U.S. citizen born abroad because of *sanguia*, or blood. They gave her a passport for me and declared me an American citizen, so I had dual citizenship. We came to the States quite a bit in my childhood, but I didn't know any English. My mother tried very desperately to get me to speak English, but I wouldn't do it as a child. I spoke only Spanish.

I grew up in Caracas and Valencia, where my grandparents lived. I remember the elections vividly. I participated as a kid, distributing fliers, putting up yard signs, and taking part in the democratic process. It was no different in Venezuela. We did a lot of the same things. One thing that was quite different was that you were either quite wealthy, or you were really very poor. I don't think there was much of a middle class. My father was a civil engineer with a Ph.D., and most people who had money were either in the oil industry, or they were engineers, professionals, or in the arts.

My mom's parents in Miami were very poor. They had no air conditioning in the house. It gets very hot and humid, and air conditioning is a real necessity; if you didn't have central air in the house, you were *poor*. For me, that was culture shock in reverse. You'd think that a Third World country would be without amenities, but it was actually the opposite for me. In Venezuela, we had comforts, and my mom had a maid and a nanny. Life was very nice for us.

I've always been a pretty big ham. I've been in the performing arts since I was three, and danced on a TV variety show for kids when I was six. I did that for about four years, and it was great. That station was one of the first television stations that Chávez shut down. That was so traumatic for me, and I couldn't believe that happened in my home.

Sadly, my dad developed inoperable cancer when I was nine and passed away. My mom decided we would move to the U.S., and we rooted ourselves here. That wasn't a problem for my mom because she was from here, but for me, I had to learn the language. I was ten, and it's easier for children to learn a second language, but still, it was a difficult experience for me. I managed to learn English pretty quickly and tried to assimilate as best I could. I understood about discrimination, and I was determined that I wouldn't let culture define me. I decided I'm going to be American, I'm going to act like an American, and this was going to be my country.

My mom and her family were all Democrats. They told me that Democrats championed poor people and minorities. My grandparents were poor, and when my mom filled out applications for free school lunches, it just freaked me out. I didn't want to do it – taking handouts just wasn't in my DNA. My grandparents told me it was okay. They really thought there was nothing wrong with government handouts, even though I instinctively knew it wasn't right.

President Reagan came to Miami when I was in middle school. I saw him on TV and I just took to him. He was unique and genuine, and listening to him changed my outlook on life, politics, everything. Much to my grandmother's dismay, I announced, "Hey guys, I'm a Republican. I don't know about the rest of you, but I'm a Republican!"

It's always been important for me to keep up with current events. Ronald Reagan had such an influence on me that when I went to college, I majored in political science. My goal was to work in D.C. as a translator, and maybe go to Venezuela. That didn't pan out because I got married and stayed in Florida. I really missed my father's family in Venezuela. Unfortunately, I never saw my favorite uncle again – he passed away when I was in college.

The situation in Venezuela in the early 1990s just went from bad to worse. They had a lot of economic problems, but they still had a democracy and capitalism. The Venezuelan currency, the Bolívar, had been devalued so horribly that the savings my late father left us had dwindled to almost nothing.

In 1998, my father's parents in Venezuela started talking about this charismatic man, Hugo Chávez. My grandfather was retired, but he still had great benefits, so they were doing okay. They were very excited about this man. It's funny, the parallels between him and Obama are really close. Chávez ran on hope and change. That was his mantra. He was going to go in there and fix the financial problems. It's funny how some dictators come into power that way. He basically befriended everybody, and he was the people's guy. He was cool, charismatic, seemed to be smart and very well-spoken. And my grandparents fell for it.

I wasn't comfortable with Chávez. I'd done some research on him. I didn't like the fact that he had a military background and had socialistic tendencies. I could see the writing on the wall, and I begged them not to vote for them. But they, along with a lot of other Venezuelans, fell for it. Here we are, eleven years later, and he's taken over the country.

My grandparents have since passed away, but one of my cousins works for the cement company in Venezuela. I emailed him in the summer of 2009, asking what the situation was like for him personally. And he said, "Oh, Rebecca, I can't talk about any of that. They'll confiscate my computer."

What? I couldn't *believe* that, and I even told him, "That's ridiculous. They can't do that."

He just said, "Yes. They can."

That was the end of it – he couldn't really talk about it. But I told him, "There is no way that could ever happen in the United States of America." About two days later, the story broke about Mark Lloyd, the FCC's Chief Diversity Officer (or Czar), praising Hugo Chávez for how he led "an incredible revolution – a democratic revolution."

I thought, "Oh, no! What am I thinking? It *can* happen here!" That's exactly how Chávez worked his way through. Basically, he shut down Radio Caracas TV's broadcast signal in 2007 with the excuse that their license had expired. RCTV had a daily opinion program that opposed him. Now, he wouldn't go in and say, "I'm a dictator, and I'm going to close you down." No, it looked like it was legal to some people. He did that, he shut them down, and I believe he's continuing to do that under the farce of the license expiration.

Recently, he went into a television station called Globovision, which is a 24-hour news station, along the lines of Fox News. They're very critical of Chávez, and he doesn't take too kindly to that. He has people called Chávistas who are basically like the Brown Shirts. They stormed the station, tear gassed it, and shut it down. Chávez said the station was inciting violence against him. It's actually happening there. Venezuela was once a beautiful, free, prosperous place, and now it's going up in smoke. It's literally going up in smoke.

A lot of people still like Chávez, which is amazing. People who believe his boloney and the poor people love him, because he has managed to take money away from all the rich people to fund government programs for the poor people. Of course, if you rob Peter to pay Paul, Paul's always going to vote for you. I believe that's the reason Chávez continually manages to be re-elected, because a majority of people like him still, because they like what socialism gives them.

Venezuela has actual democratic elections; I know that at the beginning of Chávez's presidency, they probably weren't rigging them. I don't know what's happened recently, but I just don't know if a majority of people hate him enough to vote him out. There have been a lot of protests, but it's hard for people to vote against someone if he's giving them candy. The economy there has been getting worse because of social-ism, but the poor people are dependent on the handouts. That's what I'm so afraid of in the U.S., is that the people who get all the entitlements will elect Obama again, because they like getting handouts. I'm just hoping and praying that doesn't happen here, like it did in Venezuela.

Chávez hasn't been defeated yet and he's propped up a lot of dictators. He's using his power in ways that you would think are unimaginable for an elected official. There's so much. It would take hours to read about it all. But look at Obama. Look what he's doing with all the czars, the govern-ment takeover of GM and health care, telling the banks what they should do, and the plans he announced during the cam-paign to form a civilian national security force separate from our military. That's crazy! Absolutely insane crazy, but that's exactly what Chávez did. Chávez got a civilian army.

My cousin hasn't said much because he's afraid for his job. He's afraid of what they might do to him. He has a nephew whom I've never met. He's a reporter, and he's blocked out his MySpace and other social networking sites a couple of times, talking about the threats of harassment. They recently threatened to arrest and imprison reporters. The parallels are there.

It's like a thief that comes in the middle of the night. No one expected this man to do what he's doing. Nobody thought he would take them into socialism, because Venezuela is not socialist. I guess every country can have that tendency, only because the rich and powerful can see it as an opportunity to be the elites. They can pit the poor against the business-people; it's class envy. In Venezuela, it was no different. But doctors and the health care system, that's a whole other thing. The infant mortality rate has skyrocketed, because socialized medicine doesn't work there, either.

I went through this ten years ago, seeing Chávez coming into power, seeing what he did to the country that I was born in and that I still love. And now, living through it this time, with Obama: first, the country I was born in, and now my adopted country. I thought, oh, this *can't* be happening! The parallels are just way, *way* too close. It's just scary.

I don't know if Obama is following Chávez's playbook. I do know that Obama tries to act like he isn't, but when they shook hands, I just about died. I thought, oh no he didn't! I believe that in some respects, Obama thinks that any dictator who would have socialist or Marxist tendencies is okay in his book, because that is who he is. I would have way more respect for Obama if he admitted he was a socialist, but he won't do that. He says he's doing it for us. Isn't that amazing?

They're acting straight. Chávez admitted he was a socialist and quotes Castro, but he won't ever say that he's a dictator. Never. He says, "No, the people love me. I'm an elected president, and I'm for the people. I'm for *all* of Venezuela." To hear him talk is like when you're listening to Obama, and he's acting like we're the crazy people, because he's so not-socialist, according to him. When you listen to Chávez, it's the same thing. You may not be able to understand Chávez, but he's basically saying the same thing Obama's saying. I think we have a wolf in sheep's clothing.

So, Chávez ran for president, and after his first term ended, he won again. When he ran the second time, he did have opposition trying to wake people up. Unfortunately, I don't think enough people woke up. Then, he changed the Constitution to increase his presidential term from five to six years.

Chávez tried before to change the Constitution to remove term limits, and he finally succeeded in February 2010. He can run and serve as many times as he wants as long as he gets the majority of votes. That's how he's sneaking his way into dictatorship. He was elected by popular vote, but then he changed the Constitution. In 1999, he changed the name of Venezuela as part of his "revolutionary project." It's called República Bolívariana de Venezuela. But we still call it Venezuela.

He's made so many changes to the Constitution that help him increase his power, so that he can say that whatever he's doing is legal, it's constitutional. Why? Because he changed the Constitution. Well, if Obama pushes through a constitutional change, then he can keep doing whatever he's doing, because the Constitution would be changed. If he can't do that, he still has the power of Executive Orders.

I think that Obama will probably try to do something like that on the pretext of an emergency. It's just a gut feeling I have, because Chávez did the same thing. First he duped the people into thinking he was their only hope, and now he won't leave. Everything that Chávez does is an 'emergency'.

Obama has pushed through so many programs, pushed us into such deep debt, going from one crisis to the next. I feel it's happening here, and it's just so eerie. I feel like I'm reliving it, except this time it's here. And where do you go? Of all places, this can't be happening to our country.

With Obama doing all this stuff, promoting a civilian army, forcing government health care on us, talking about controlling the Internet in an emergency, who knows what he'll do with illegal immigration? What if he pushes amnesty? They're poor, so they'll tip the scales again.

Obama can't seem to give a speech without the teleprompter, for sure. And when I listen to Chávez speak, he makes me sick. Other people who listen to him think he's a god and think he only wants the best for Venezuela. What's so interesting about these two men is how they affect people who have been indoctrinated.

Talking about social justice, redistributing wealth – I think it makes it easier for somebody who believes in that to vote for somebody like Barack Obama. They see him as this guy who was brought up on the wrong side of the tracks, and who went through so much without knowing his father. What a nice Cinderella story. Well, they're missing the whole point.

He was raised pretty well and went to good schools. Yes, it would be great if somebody did that legitimately, but Obama has so many skeletons in his closet. Not only that, he doesn't believe in what Reagan believed. He doesn't believe that people should get off the couch, get off the entitlement mentality, and work hard and fight for the American dream. He doesn't believe that. That makes people free and independent, and that makes them a threat to his power. He's trying to keep the poor where they are, blaming others, because if they *really* succeed, they won't need him anymore.

The administration wants the poor people right where they are. Yes, they'll give them handouts, but that's the extent of it. I don't think they want them to get out of the barrios or the projects. That's when I cringe, because people who drink the Kool-Aid just don't see this man for what he is. And especially what hurts is that so many Latinos voted for him, and they're the very people that he's trying to keep down. And it's sickening, it really is.

When I heard that as a State Senator in Illinois, Obama voted against the Born Alive Act – just allowing a baby who survived an abortion to live – I was just sick. His mentors were radicals, so far beyond where liberals are. That's also the thing with Chávez: His mentors were all socialists, too. You are what you believe, who you keep around you.

These two men are in two different worlds, but they share the same ideology. I think that's why he uses a teleprompter when talking about normal American issues, but when he talks to unions or progressive groups, the words come easily because he believes them. When he told Joe the Plumber it was good to "spread the wealth around," that was from his heart. That came easily.

We need to get our country back on the right track. I think we can't afford to have him serve another term. If he does, then we're going to be in the same boat Venezuela's in. I believe it in my heart. When he said he would be happy to be a single-term president, I wondered, how long is the term going to be? I fear that's his agenda. If he really wanted to be re-elected, do you think he would be irking the center and right of this country like this? He knows he can't win an election like this.

There are several scenarios. Either he's really dumb and just doesn't get it, or he knows exactly what he's doing. And he is either setting up these programs that would be impossible to eliminate, or he's fixing it so he won't have to run again, because that's what Chávez did... exactly that. Even though there's a great majority of poor people in Venezuela, I don't know that they *all* like him. I suspect there's a great percentage that do, but I think the right in Venezuela really tried hard to get people to realize what kind of person he is, that he's not giving them opportunity and freedom like they want.

So, I think that Chávez changing the Constitution so he never has to run again is the same reason I'm worried that Obama might want to do that. I don't know. I can't imagine how anyone in their right mind would alienate the majority of this country and expect to be re-elected. And if he only expects to be a one-term president, like he said, why is he doing so much damage? Why are they doing everything so fast?

It really bothered me when Obama said in an interview that the Bill of Rights was a document of negative liberties, casting doubt on our founding documents. Glenn Beck really hit it on the head about the czars and how the administration follows the progressives. I've only listened to him for a couple of years, but he just called it. Everything that he has said has happened. My mom says, "Honey, do you think he could just be making it up?"

I told her, "Mom, you don't understand. I've listened to him for over two years now, and he's never been wrong."

She said that gave her chills. You know, that's the thing. If you know Glenn Beck, the man speaks the truth. He's already been to hell and back. He knows what it's like to be at the bottom – nothing scares him. But he knows our country is headed for a terrible direction.

I don't know if Obama will go as far as Chávez did, but he's got a lot of cronies. I don't know how that parallels the czars, because you have a congress in Venezuela, too, but these people aren't in Congress. When Obama started getting all these czars, I immediately thought, my gosh, he's doing what Chávez did. I just don't see how people can't see that pa-rallel. I don't believe that Obama's mentality is pro-American, not the way we've always known it.

I know that Chávez surrounded himself with his cronies since his first term, and they've been with him since then. How he got them, I don't know. My grandparents were pretty apolitical, so it's not easy trying to get stuff out of them. I read the online Spanish networks, and it's really difficult to see what he's done. He hides it well, and I know he won't call them Commissars, or whatever, just like the White House got on Beck because he called them czars. It's the same thing.

But really and truly, what set me off was when Mark Lloyd praised Chávez and his "incredible revolution" – shutting down the stations that challenged him. I thought, *What?!* You didn't just say that. It just boggles my mind that Obama can have somebody like that be the Diversity Officer of the FCC. How in the world can you have somebody serving in that capacity who believes that what Chávez did was great? There are just so many things being thrown at us right now.

Although Venezuela was a capitalist country, it had a *lot* of poverty, much more than we have in the U.S. That may be the difference between the two countries, that Chávez pits the poor against the rich to stay in power. The numbers are there – I think the poverty rate is around 80 percent. It's huge.

I think that when you look at the population in this country versus Venezuela, that's where the differences are. We do have a middle class in the United States, even though they're trying to squelch the middle class. And we have people who woke up. We saw the writing on the wall, where we're not going to let this happen. You can see this with the Tea Parties, the town hall meetings, and just the ordinary citizens who are melting down the congressional switchboards.

Venezuelans just now are starting to push back, but they don't have the majority. They don't have a large enough population like we have, because the United States is basically center-right. Because of that, I think we have a distinct advantage that the Venezuelans, unfortunately, don't have. If 20 percent of the population is conservative and pro-capitalism, and 80 percent is poor and more liberal – the scales are not in the conservatives' favor. I believe they *are* in our favor in the United States, if we can do something about it and not give up.

Monument in Caracas, inscribed with
the names of Venezuela's founding fathers:
José Leonardo Chirinos and Francisco de Miranda.
(Photo: Courtesy Rebecca S.)

EPILOGUE

THE GENERAL PERCEPTION IS that writers teach, and readers learn, whenever a printed piece is created. However, the creation of *Pursuing Liberty* was quite different. The true teachers are the immigrants who graciously shared their stories; the writers are mostly just conduits of their thoughts to the readers. In this case, we learned a tremendous amount along the way.

Not all of these lessons were comfortable, some were downright ominous. It didn't take long at all, when compiling the histories of our subject immigrants, for eerie patterns to emerge. Patterns of government subjugation of people all over the world emerged, in almost identical fashions. Patterns that are uncomfortably familiar when overlaid upon America's recent history.

It's easy to dismiss these concerns as simple paranoia of right-wing extremists, but the fact remains that Americans have lost a tremendous amount of personal freedoms in the last few decades. For example, private property rights are being increasingly usurped by local planning boards, air travelers are scrutinized and assumed guilty until they prove themselves harmless enough to board a commercial aircraft, and our proud but messy early American history is disappearing from the curricula of public schools. At first, these items seem unrelated, but they all share the common attribute of a growing general distrust of average American. And it gets worse.

As our state and federal governments steadily introduce new social programs, "entitlements," and unfunded mandates wrapped in the guise of compassion, the burden on the public treasury becomes severe. The inevitable result is that average taxpayers are impressed into increasing economic slavery to the state, where the fruits of their labors are withheld in ever-increasing amounts. And they have no choice in the matter.

The experiences of our featured immigrants should send a shiver up the spine of any reader who has been paying attention to recent American events. These brave souls all left deteriorating or intolerable conditions in their homelands, for the promise of all of the freedoms and opportunity that America has traditionally offered. And now they wonder, without exception: What is happening to my new country? Why does this feel so familiar?

The sad fact is that there is no better place to go from here. There is not another, better, freer America to which to emigrate. We have no other choice but to dig in our heels and stand and fight for our disappearing birthright. We owe nothing less to future generations of Americans.

Cory Emberson
Rick Lindstrom
2010

AUTHORS' NOTES

IT'S EASY TO SIT BACK and bemoan the expansion of government and the loss of personal freedom that we've personally witnessed. It doesn't take much work at all to find examples occurring with increasing frequency in our lives. And there are many in the new media who indulge in this, preaching to a receptive, mostly conservative choir that finds some solace in hearing from those with similar political perspectives.

Not too long ago, these voices were pretty rare in the mainstream media, as traditional newspapers and broadcast networks slowly drifted farther to the left without challenge. I began to doubt my own perception of reality, for what I had seen during my first four decades was now at odds with the messages, both subtle and blatant, I got from TV, radio, newspapers, and film. I seriously considered finding a therapist to "fix" whatever was wrong with me. My salvation came when a local radio station switched formats and became talk radio. Suddenly, I knew two things: My perceptions weren't wrong, and I was no longer alone in my beliefs.

This unprecedented radio programming change was happening to stations all across the country, and finding receptive audiences who were starving for an alternative to NPR and other public radio outlets. Soon, conservative websites and blogs began appearing, and the traditional media no longer had a lock on managing the public's perceptions.

It's been almost twenty years since the on-air talent at San Francisco's KSFO saved my sanity, and the subsequent national success of Rush Limbaugh, Sean Hannity, Mark Levin, Glenn Beck, and the Fox News network underscores the continuing demand from the public. Of course, left-leaning outlets such as the now-defunct Air America, were rushed to the air to counter the perspective of the right.

After watching various media outlets become more politically polarized, I can now see how the left was so successful at isolating and marginalizing those who hold conservative viewpoints, to the point where those on the right began to question their whole belief system. In a liberal Mecca like the San Francisco Bay Area, or in Manhattan, or Austin, or Boulder, or Santa Cruz, or Seattle (pick a city), the targeting, isolation, and destruction of conservative thought in society at large is *de rigueur*. I witnessed this first-hand when I lived in Berkeley, California, for six years in the early 1970s. And for many who live there now, it's still 1968, and protesting "the Man" has become a way of life spanning decades.

As tempting as it may be to define America's recently declining freedoms as a left versus right issue, I think it runs much deeper than that. No matter what side of the political fence you may place yourself, freedom and liberty are cherished by all. I find it highly ironic that those who have dreams of a perfect socialist utopia, those who wish to force all Americans into their vision of the American dream, are the greatest beneficiaries of those unique freedoms passed down to them from past generations of patriots.

Many of the countries they wish to emulate here in America would not tolerate such freedom of speech and thought for a second. If there's one common thread that runs through the narratives of those who've escaped such repressive regimes worldwide, it's the clear recognition that America is still the last, best hope for liberty on earth.

Which brings us to the point of how we can effectively work to restore America to a society that works for the interests of the people, instead of demanding more in taxes while placing further restrictions on the freedoms of the average citizen. The Founding Fathers had it right then, and it's still right now: We have a sacred duty as Americans to rein in any government that has grown out of control.

It ain't gonna be easy. But the work has already started with a flood of fellow Americans getting personally involved and not staying quiet anymore. The success of the many Tea Party movements nationwide underscores just how deep this passion runs, where hard-working, tax-paying, average citizens have finally found their voices again. As much as the mass media would like to pretend these people are nut jobs or simply don't exist, the new Internet-based media is rife with good old-fashioned American patriotism that has been cowed into silence for way too long.

So, I'd like to offer a few simple tips to those who are just as lost as I was two decades ago. Considering them won't hurt at all, and you just might feel better in the morning.

Tip One: Have Faith

In our increasingly secular society, the word "faith" has been under attack lately. But it's still an important commodity, and it comes in many different varieties. One of the most important kinds of faith is the simple belief in your own convictions. Assuming that your parent(s) raised you to have ethics and to know the difference between right and wrong, it's important to not give in to the temptation of transitory political fads at the expense of your integrity. Stick to your guns.

Another important kind of faith is the confidence that your fellow Americans aren't all as dumb as our politicians would like us to believe. The wisdom of the average American has stood the test of time for well over two hundred years, and always comes through to pull the fat out of the fire when the decisions of self-serving politicos backfire and jeopardize us all. As a whole, Americans are still interested in leaving the country in better shape for our children and their children, and expressing a bit of faith in their basic goodness is something that most self-anointed politicians still haven't gotten the hang of.

Of course, faith in a higher power isn't a bad thing, no matter what the mass media claims. It's also true that this country was founded on the core values found in Christian-Judeo ethics, which are also the basis for our judicial system. A certain amount of faith is needed to understand that America is a nation of laws, not of men, and to understand the difference between the two.

Tip Two: Know Your Rights

W.C. Fields once observed that "You can't cheat an honest man," and he was on to something. You also can't cheat, or easily overthrow, an honest government. Once a government body places that first foot on the slippery slope of situational ethics, class warfare, oppressive taxation, selective law enforcement, self-enrichment, cronyism, or myriad other temptations, the pressure to crack down on the citizenry to keep them in line becomes intense.

Knowing your rights has several facets. There are rights that are bestowed by the Creator (whomever you choose that to be), and are not the legitimate province of man nor government to abrogate or withhold. (This doesn't keep them from trying, however.)

It's also helpful to know the rights, or powers, that are legitimately bestowed upon our governments with the consent of the governed (that's us). These specific powers are spelled out in our Constitution, which serves to limit what powers our federal government can assume. Contrary to a popular, but incorrect, thought that seems to be gaining acceptance, the American federal government cannot bestow "rights" upon itself, and it is still bound by the Constitution.

A good way to get a refresher in how our state and federal governments were intended to work for the benefit of the governed is a quick review of our Constitution and its first Ten Amendments (the Bill of Rights). Even though the original language is a bit dated, they are straightforward and easily understandable. And having personal knowledge of your rights is Kryptonite to those who depend on our ignorance to press their tyranny upon us.

Tip Three: Involvement

Just the thought of trying to find the time or energy to devote to another cause is daunting, especially when our lives are already overloaded with everyday obligations and commitments. What's frequently overlooked is the symbiosis that occurs when like-minded individuals join forces and work toward a common goal. This is reason enough to seek out fellow patriots, even if it's just to compare notes and spend a few minutes chatting. It's rare to come away from such interactions with less energy than you started with.

However, the serious side of involvement is that it can't be delegated to someone else. The far left in this country has had over a century to refine its game plan for the destruction of our exceptional society. America has long been the needle in the eye of those who want to see global governance, and who'd like to eliminate the proof that a capitalist system can and does work toward creating a higher standard of living for everybody. With very few exceptions, the "poor" in our country enjoy indoor plumbing, heating and air conditioning, multiple vehicles, health care (even if they can't afford it), food stamps, education, government-provided stipends, and a dizzying list of other benefits.

This level of public assistance comes with a crippling price, however, and more and more people are becoming dependent on fewer and fewer taxpayers. The only way to keep our heirs from a lifetime of servicing our ever-increasing debt is to rein in the government juggernaut that is spending all of us, and our kids, into the poorhouse. We may not completely agree on the best way to take corrective action, but the first step is gaining public realization that this is the most crucial situation facing the security of Americans and successive generations today.

Tip Four: Have Courage

Are you worried about offending someone, somewhere when you express your thoughts, even if you know them to be valid? Are you worried what others might think of you if you say something outside what's popular or considered "normal"? Are you hesitant to express any sort of comment or criticism of someone who richly deserves it, if they happen to be anything but an Anglo, Christian male?

What is commonly known as "political correctness" has stifled free speech more effectively than any society that George Orwell could have possibly envisioned. And worse, almost any verbal expression regarding someone in a "protected group" that's not positive can even lead to charges of hate speech if an activist lawyer gets involved. The old truism of "sticks and stones" we learned as children has been replaced by the concept of "fighting words" as a defense of violent acts in response to being "dissed."

This is madness. As a society, we have become so tolerant, so polite, so eager not to offend anybody, that we've essentially allowed ourselves to be intimidated into silence. And political opportunists, ever vigilant for something to use as a wedge issue, now depend on this silence to further their activism.

However, we still do have constitutional rights as individuals. We still have the right to express ourselves without fear of recrimination. But to do this today takes a little courage and belief in yourself. Talk to your friends about things you see going wrong. Discuss what you see on the news or read in the paper. Compare the reality that's being portrayed with your own life experiences. Take the time to research the motives behind any new government proposals, and investigate the backgrounds of those who are keen to see it come to fruition. Power and money are life's two biggest corrupting influences, and we've seen all too often how well-meaning people who want to do good for the world can fall prey to a scheme that's based in self-enrichment and an ugly quest for power and influence.

Books like this one can serve to raise a red flag and increase awareness over a particular issue. But once the words have been printed, they're not likely to change on demand.

However, the Internet has become a powerful tool in communicating with like-minded citizens, and it's constantly being updated to reflect the latest in societal changes. If you're not using the Internet now to stay involved and connected, I would strongly recommend learning just a few basic computer skills that will allow you do so. If nothing else, you'll gain new confidence in your thinking with your new-found online friends.

It's always come down to the common man to overcome tyranny. Although we hire our leaders to look after our best interests, they often fail miserably once they lose the connection with those they purport to represent. And as sure as the sun rises in the east, it's up to us to grab the helm and set a new course.

Once the people show the way, the "leaders" will follow.

—Rick Lindstrom

March 2010

PURSUING LIBERTY WAS BORN while I was on hold. Frustrated with the disparity between what I saw and heard in the media, and what my own eyes and ears were telling me, I'd taken to occasionally calling talk host Brian Sussman's evening show on KSFO in San Francisco on my way home.

One evening in October 2008, I waited my turn. Alex was a regular caller who had come to America from the former Soviet Union, and what he said froze my blood: "Please, don't do this. Don't elect Obama. He says he's a moderate, but he's not. I've heard these words before. I've heard this song before. It always ends badly. That's why I left. I came to America to escape Communism. If America isn't free any more, where do I go?"

What could I have possibly said to follow that? Alex said it all, and it became inescapable that a collection of these stories needed to be published.

We wrote *Pursuing Liberty* for everyone. While the people whose stories are told here have very strong opinions about the state of current events in the United States, their objections, concerns, and unease are borne of principles, not political parties. I agree. It truly is about what's right, not who's right.

Those who would undermine our unassailable rights to self-determination benefit when we turn our attention from them to each other. It's a game of "Let's you and him fight" writ large, and it's a losing game for all of us. At the end of that game, we'll find that through inattention, political hostility and distraction, and plain old exhaustion, our inalienable rights will have been diluted, weakened, and distorted into the very political systems of repression that our newest Americans rejected.

It's become a cliché that we don't appreciate what we've been born into: the freest nation God graced humanity with. The cold reality is, if we aren't aware of what people are willing to leave to be free – and how it came to be that way – we're in real danger of giving it away. Anything we might gain in exchange – security, being relieved of the responsibility of our own lives, strings-attached entitlements from an increasingly centralized government – will never be worth it.

Just about everyone has a personal connection to our country's foundation of liberty. On my father's side, one of my direct ancestors was Arthur Middleton, one of the signers of the Declaration of Independence from Charleston, South

Carolina. He was a bold thinker, and a leader of the Council of Safety, which oversaw the local militias. When Charleston was taken by the British in 1780, he and two other signers from South Carolina, Edward Rutledge and Thomas Heyward, Jr., were held for nearly a year as prisoners of war in St. Augustine, Florida. At the end of the war, they returned to find their property stolen and destroyed by the British. It's not surprising to learn that despite his British birth, Middleton was no fan of the Loyalists on American soil.

Almost everyone knows the final line of the Declaration: "And for the support of this Declaration with a firm reliance on the protection of divine providence, we mutually pledge to each other our lives, our fortunes, and our sacred honor." That was no idle promise, meant for a public relations boost. It was both a statement of fact and a solemn promise that they would ultimately fulfill.

To our detriment, the critical decisions and very real personal dangers that our Founders and their families undertook in the defense of liberty have often been relegated to glancing lessons in school, too often dismissed as the irrelevant experiences of "dead white men." This is more than a shame: It's a danger to the continued existence of a free citizenry, to our ability to determine our own fate.

Which brings me to my mother's father, Samuel Peizer. He was born in Vilnius in the late 1800s – it was in Poland at the time – and at age eight, was sent to America. The specific reasons for his emigration are unknown to me, but he had ten other siblings, and his father, a teacher, surely knew that the opportunity for a better, freer life awaited him in the United States. The view of the Statue of Liberty depicted on this book's cover is the view seen from ships approaching Ellis Island in New York Harbor. It's a view of opportunity, not guarantees.

These two men, Founder and immigrant, share an everlasting bond. It's the same bond that each of us – American by birth or by choice – will always possess: that of liberty. It's our right, and our obligation, to actively and continually protect and defend it as Americans standing together.

There were many startling lessons gained from these stories of flight from oppression: how tyranny begins, often with a whisper; the depths to which a government corrupted by absolute power will sink to seize control of its citizens; and the brutality and inhumanity with which it will try to retain that power. The most astonishing lesson, however, is the one that will ultimately cause the failure of repression everywhere on Earth: the unconquerable craving for freedom in the hearts of the oppressed.

Even someone who's known only tyranny knows in his soul that is not how his life was meant to be. Freedom is the natural state of man. It's up to us to protect it, always.

—Cory Emberson
March 2010

CITATIONS

1. SOVIET UNION

Halperin, Micah. "Josef Stalin: Short, Paranoid, and Insecure."
   In *Thugs: How history's most notorious despots transformed
   the world through terror, tyranny, and mass murder.* 242-9.
   Nashville: Thomas Nelson, 2007.

Litwin, Peter. "The Russian Revolution." EURO 344, Spring
   2002, http://depts.washington.edu/baltic/papers/
   russianrevolution.htm.

Systems SpetsNaz, http://www.systemaspetsnaz.com/
   russian_history.htm.

Travel Guide to Russia: Welcome to the New Russia.
   http://www.geographia.com/Russia.

2. POLAND

Polonia Today: A Brief History of Poland.
   http://www.poloniatoday.com/historyix.htm.

Timeline Poland. http://timelines.ws/countries/POLAND.HTML.

3. ITALY

Execution of Mussolini. October 25, 2008.
   http://www.custermen.com/ItalyWW2/ILDUCE/
   Mussolini.htm.

Goldberg, Jonah. "Mussolini: The Father of Fascism." In
   *Liberal Fascism: The secret history of the American left, from
   Mussolini to the politics of change.* 1-52. New York: Broadway
   Books, 2007, 2009.

Halperin, Micah. "Benito Mussolini: He Who Kept The Trains on Time." In *Thugs: How history's most notorious despots transformed the world through terror, tyranny, and mass murder.* 200-6. Nashville: Thomas Nelson, 2007.

Timeline: Italy. http://timelines.ws/countries/ITALYA.HTML, http://timelines.ws/countries/ITALYB.HTML.

Truehorn, Chris. History Learning Site: Italy 1900 to 1939: March on Rome. http://www.historylearningsite.co.uk/march_on_rome.htm.

4. IRAQ

BBC ON THIS DAY, March 16, 1988.: Thousands die in Halabja gas attack. http://news.bbc.co.uk/onthisday/hi/dates/stories/march/16/newsid_4304000/4304853.stm.

Central Intelligence Agency. The World Factbook: Iraq. http://www.cia.gov/library/publications/the-world-factbook/geos/iz.html.

Halperin, Micah. "Saddam Hussein: Dean of the Demons." In *Thugs: How history's most notorious despots transformed the world through terror, tyranny, and mass murder.* 146-52. Nashville: Thomas Nelson, 2007.

History of Iraq: Timeline of Events, 6750 BCE – 2004 CE. http://atheism.about.com/library/FAQs/Islam/countries/blis_iraq_chron.htm.

History Timelines. http://www.history-timelines.org/uk/places-timelines/24-iraq-timeline.htm.

Iraq is sovereign. http://en.wikisource.org/wiki/Iraq_is_sovereign.

Iraq Timeline. http://news.bbc.co.uk/2/hi/middle_east/
737483.stm.

Saddam Captured 'Like a Rat' in Raid. (December 14, 2003)
http://www.foxnews.com/story/0,2933,105706,00.html.

Saddam 'caught like a rat' in a hole. (December 15, 2003)
http://www.cnn.com/2003/WORLD/meast/12/14/sprj.irq.sadd
am.operation/index.html.

Times Online. "Halabja, the massacre the West tried to
ignore."(January 18, 2010) http://www.timesonline.co.uk/
tol/news/world/iraq/article6991512.ece.

5. IRAN

Beale, Jonathan. "Obama's cautious reaction to Iran." BBC
News, Washington. (June 16, 2009) http://news.bbc.co.uk/
2/hi/8102061.stm.

Central Intelligence Agency. The World Factbook: Iran.
www.cia.gov/library/publications/the-world-factbook/
geos/ir.html.

Halperin, Micah. "Mohammad Reza Pahlavi: Brutal Oppres-
sor, Political Ally." In *Thugs: How history's most notorious
despots transformed the world through terror, tyranny, and
mass murder.* 92-6. Nashville: Thomas Nelson, 2007.

Ibid. "Ali Khamenei: Supreme Leader Jr.". 110-4.

Lahidji, Abdol-karim. "Legal Status of Non-Muslims in Iran."
Rozaneh Magazine (Nov.-Dec.2003). Vol. XIX, Nos. 1-2.
http://www.rozanehmagazine.com/NovDec03/
anonmuslim.html.

"Obama's Iran Abdication" Review and Outlook: *Wall Street Journal* (June 18, 2009) http://online.wsj.com/article/ SB124520170103721579.html.

On The Matrix: Timeline of Persian/Iranian History: www.on-the-matrix.com/mideast/IranTimeline.aspx.

Rubin, Marc. "Obama's tepid response to Iran." (June 18, 2009). Examiner.com San Francisco. http://www.examiner.com/x-6572-NY-Obama-Administration-Examiner~y2009m6d18-Obamas-spineless-response-to-Iran.

Timeline: Iran. http://timelines.ws/countries/IRAN.HTML. http://timelines.ws/countries/IRAN_2005_10.HTML.

6. VIETNAM

Amnesty International. "Vietnam: Father Thadeus Nguyen Van Ly – Prisoner of Conscience." (July 4, 2001) http://www.amnesty.org/en/library/info/ASA41/005/2001.

Timeline: Vietnam. http://timelines.ws/countries/VIETNAMA.HTML. http://timelines.ws/countries/VIETNAMB.HTML.

7. CUBA

Fontova, Humberto. "The Bay of Pigs – An Anniversary of Heroism and Shame." Townhall.com (April 13, 2010). http://townhall.com/columnists/HumbertoFontova/ 2010/04/13/the_bay_of_pigs%E2%80%94an_anniversary_ of_heroism_and_shame.

Kennedy, John F. The Bay of Pigs Invasion Speech: Address to the American Society of Newspaper Editors." (April 20,

1961) http://www.famousquotes.me.uk/speeches/
John_F_Kennedy/7.htm.

Timeline: Cuba. http://timelines.ws/countries/CUBA.HTML.

8. VENEZUELA

Cartaginese, Claude. *David Horowitz's News Real Blog.* "Hugo
Chávez's Socialism: The Little Engine That Couldn't." (January 12, 2010) http://www.newsrealblog.com/2010/
01/12/hugo-chavez%E2%80%99s-socialism-the-little-engine-
that-couldn%E2%80%99t/.

FOXNews.com. "Chávez urges Obama to turn to socialism."
(March 7, 2009) http://www.foxnews.com/politics/2009/
03/07/chavez-urges-obama-turn-socialism/.

Halperin, Micah. *Thugs: How history's most notorious despots
transformed the world through terror, tyranny, and mass
murder.* Thomas Nelson, 2007.

International Business Times. "Chávez wins vote eliminating
presidential term limits in Venezuela." (February 16, 2009)
http://www.ibtimes.com/articles/20090216/venezuela-
hugo-chavez-presidential-term.htm.

Lonely Planet: Venezuela History.
http://www.lonelyplanet.com/venezuela/history.

Ria Novosti. "Venezuela's leader seeks unlimited presidential
terms. (July 13, 2007) http://en.rian.ru/world/
20070713/68889242.html.

Timeline: Venezuela. http://timelines.ws/countries/
VENEZUELA.HTML.

USA Today (January 10, 2007) http://www.usatoday.com/
news/world/2007-01-10-chavez-venezuela_x.htm)

973.04
EMB

LaVergne, TN USA
16 November 2010
205059LV00003B/83/P